Jane Hunter

AMERICA AT WAR:

The Home Front, 1941–1945

D0925393

RICHARD POLENBERG (Ph.D., Columbia University),
editor of this volume in the
Eyewitness Accounts of American History series,
is Associate Professor of American History
at Cornell University.
He is the author of
Reorganizing Roosevelt's Government, 1936-1939.

AMERICA AT WAR:

The Home Front, 1941–1945

edited by

Richard Polenberg

A SPECTRUM BOOK

PRENTICE-HALL, Inc., *Englewood Cliffs, N. J.*

Copyright © 1968 by PRENTICE-HALL, INC., Englewood Cliffs, N. J. All rights reserved. No part of this book may be reproduced in any form or by any means without permission in writing from the publisher. *Library of Congress Catalog Card Number: 68-17822.* Printed in the United States of America.

Current Printing (last digit):
10 9 8 7 6 5 4 3 2

FOR MY MOTHER AND FATHER

Preface

The home front during World War II has not yet received a fair share of historical attention. With a few notable exceptions, students of the period have dwelt upon military exploits, foreign relations, and scientific developments leading to construction of the atomic bomb. Yet the war, as many at the time realized, had a profound impact upon the economic, political, and social structure of American society. This book of source readings is designed to aid in understanding the problems created by total war, the way in which these problems were met, and the nature of the changes in American life fostered or hastened by the war.

At the start, it may be useful to suggest some questions concerning the American experience in World War II. First, war creates a need for national unity. But how does a democratic society go about building cohesion; what techniques does it use; what obstacles does it face; and what degree of success is possible? The bitter class rivalries of the 1930's rendered the problem of healing social conflict unusually acute. Second, war transformed the American economy and brought prosperity after long years of stagnation. What was the role of government intervention in this process; to what extent were the conflicting claims of various interest groups reconciled; and what lasting changes in business, labor, and agriculture resulted? Third, the war brought about a regrouping of political forces. Were Republicans and Democrats drawn together or driven apart; who stood to gain from a suspension of partisanship; and how did the war influence the movement for social reform? A fourth set of issues concerns civil liberties and civil rights. How did the record compare with World War I; what accounted for the tolerance shown certain minority groups and the intolerance exhibited toward others; and what impact did the war have on patterns of race relations? Fifth, one might look into the effects of war upon family life and examine the social consequences of unprecedented mobility and the employment of women and children. Finally, because the war altered Americans' conception of their role in world affairs, it seems proper to evaluate the conflicting positions in the debate over war aims.

Each chapter in this book is concerned with one of these broad areas of inquiry, but many of the questions are complex and may undoubtedly be answered in different ways. One advantage of bringing together contemporary descriptions of events—such as Thurgood Marshall's account of a race riot—as well as representative statements of political and economic beliefs—such as David E. Lilienthal's view of social reform in wartime—is that the reader has some opportunity to come to his own conclusions and make independent evaluations. This approach may also encourage further research into American participation in World War II.

Contents

Chapter 1   **The Quest for Unity**

Chapter 2   The War Economy

Chapter 3   Politics in Wartime

1 The Quest for Unity

THE BENEFITS OF WAR

Most Americans were outraged by the Japanese attack on Pearl Harbor, but for a number of citizens war came as something of a relief, if for no other reason than that it brought an end to uncertainty. In retrospect, it seemed to E. B. White that the period from 1939 to 1941 was analogous to the time spent in a doctor's waiting room; one knew it had to end, and was relieved when it did. Others claimed that war would have its positive aspects. Recognizing the brutal and destructive consequences of war, they nevertheless affirmed that it had certain compensations: it would spread technical skills, turn people away from self-seeking, revive a sense of community, and reveal the nation's essential virility. Pointing out the advantages of war might also serve to bolster national confidence.

1 ★ Jonathan Daniels, "The Hour of Elation"

Jonathan Daniels was editor of the Raleigh, North Carolina, News and Observer. In 1942, he became Assistant Director of the Office of Defense Mobilization, and a year later Administrative Assistant to President Roosevelt. Daniels presumed that the outbreak of war marked the beginning of a new era and predicted what its tone might be. [The Nation, CLIII (December 20, 1941), 643. Reprinted by permission of The Nation.]

It is not hard to scare me. Say "Boo" and I'll jump. I don't like little unfamiliar noises in the dark. But it is going to take me a long time to be afraid about the essential strength and the essential security of America. Plenty of people have been scared in America. The first people who came to it were timid on a sea reputed to be full of monsters. The little people in the little boats who came slowly to fill its wilderness from one sea to another were frightened in the dark the big trees made and in the disturbing brightness which filled the prairies. They jumped and scurried. At Lexington and Concord the shots heard round the world began a six years' war. Bull Run was the Union's rout, from which Congressmen tumbled still running into Washington. But beyond terror, we have also and always been a people terrible in strength. We still are.

An American really doubtful today about the security of a republic which sprawls across a whole continent, full of half the riches of the world and the richest people in skills and strength on this earth, is not only a rabbit but a silly rabbit. There are some such native rabbits. Some have seen planes in empty skies. A good many of them poured stocks into a market of panic without once wondering where they would put the money they were paid except in the great, sound investment of America. Where is a dollar worth anything except in the destiny of America? Where on this earth is a life worth anything but in that destiny? When could there ever be a better time to be an American than in an hour when an American has the privilege to stand up to the full meaning of that word.

The sailors who manned the clipper ships are not gone. Our farms and cities are full of them. The craftsmen who turned the first wheels crowd the greatest industrial plant on earth. The fighting men did not die with our fathers. Our destiny did not play out when we began to play an arrogant game with dollars. The poor are not new, nor the slanders about them. The big, strong, restless, seeking poor move now as they have always moved. The country boys, the street boys have never been truly caught in dead-end streets or on lanes which just petered out in the pasture. They moved with the destiny of America. Death is not new among us any more than the willingness to die has disappeared. There are hard hands, hard heads, hearts willing to be tough between our oceans, on ships upon them and on islands, in planes in the old, old sky. Lusty, strong men and women, we are not a rabble but a race. The time has not gone in which we are willing to play with destiny for beers, or to fight in its name for a better world.

There never could have been a time when it was a greater privilege to be an American than now. The twenties are gone with self-indulgence. The thirties have disappeared with self-pity. The forties are here in which Americans stand on a continent as men—men again fighting in the crudest man terms—for ourselves and also for that destination in decency for all men of which our settlement, our spreading, was always a symbol. In an America grown magnificently male again we have a chance to fight for a homeland with the full meaning of homeland as a world that is fit to be the home of man.

Fear at such a time? It is the hour for elation. Here is the time when a man can be what an American means, can fight for what America has always meant—an audacious, adventurous seeking for a decent earth. The gullies in our earth mark not only our waste but our labor. The slums in our cities are where we stumbled when our strongest folk in peacefulness sometimes grew fat. All the weak, bad things are only shadows beside our destiny now.

No people have done so much to light the dark places at home. Sometimes we seemed to build bridges and schoolhouses while other nations built ships and planes. Sometimes we seemed to think of the poor while others thought only of soldiers. That is not loss now. That emphasis in our peace is still the emphasis in our war. That aim at home is the basis of our strength in the world. The American dream for people is still what underlies the irresistible power of our arms. That American dream is a world force now, the force of men whose whole history has been a movement toward the chance of freedom, even if they had to seize it from the wilderness, subdue a continent to secure it. No frontier is shut on that freedom-seeking spirit. Aroused now, we can show a strength which will not only mean terrible war but the possibility of a splendid peace.

We are alive—rudely wakened. That is not basis for fear but sign that our destiny survives. We are men again in America.

2 ★ *Stuart Chase,* "The Salesman's Era"

The author of many popular studies of the American economy, including The Tragedy of Waste *(1925) and* Rich Land, Poor Land *(1936), Stuart Chase had long been concerned with the way in which economic forces shaped American values. He reasoned that the effect of war upon the "American culture pattern" would be beneficial.* [Common Sense, *XI (May 1942), 160. Reprinted by permission of the author.]*

We have been off our foundation since the last war. Before 1917, or thereabouts, we lived in an age of scarcity, where goods were valued because they were hard to make, and there was no great surplus of them. I can still see my grandfather, for all he was a banker, meticulously winding balls of second-hand string. During the war, mass production came into its own, and with the 1920's we entered the age of abundance. This label does not mean that all Americans had enough material goods, only that the capacity to produce goods outstripped the purchasing power available to take them off the market. So the major job shifted from making things to selling them. The cult of "service," of the boosters and boomers, really went to town. And money—that curious man-made flow of abstract numbers—began to take precedence over goods, over men, over ethics, over everything. Mr. Bruce Barton identified Jesus as our first salesman.

With the solemn admonition from the highest quarters to sell our way through life, we were bound to lose contact with our foundations. As early as 1920, Sinclair Lewis faithfully recorded the breach in the melancholy history of George F. Babbitt. The breach gaped wider as the stock market soared to its Himalayan heights of September 1929—with Radio Common at 540.

The depression sobered some of us, but not all of us. It has taken the war to bring the era of the higher salesmanship to an end. The age of scarcity is here again. You cannot buy one new automobile tire for one million dollars. You cannot win the war with twenty trillion dollars. You can win it only with trained men, tanks, planes and ships. The numbers float through our heads, the pieces of stamped paper drop from our hands, the clank of bookkeeping machines in the cathedral halls of banks is all but meaningless. Hitler had no money, but great powers reel before his army and his air force. The Japanese were bankrupt, but where are Hong Kong, Manila, Singapore, Batavia, Rangoon and Bataan? The sun is low in the west, and it is time we put first things first.

The era of the salesman was inevitable; we were all touched with it. Brilliant writers were willing to write advertising copy that secretly nauseated them. We had to go through with it, but now it is over, dead, done and decomposing. Historians will look at the yellowing ads in *The Saturday Evening Post*, at the text books of professors of merchandising, at the build-up for Mr. Grover Whalen, at the verbal blandishments of the pain and beauty boys, at the monographs of counsels on public relations, at the homilies of Arthur Brisbane, Ivy Lee, Roger Babson, B. C. Forbes—and marvel that such dream-stuff could ever have been taken seriously.

Worse than the words were the acts. It became almost an ethical compulsion to get away with it, to put it over, to make a killing; to push one's fellow citizens down as one climbed up; to phoney and fake one's way to the top. Read "What Makes Sammy Run." Consider the monstrous indecency of door-to-door canvassing, where the kindly instinct of hospitality was deliberately exploited to sell the housewife things she had no use for. It is hard to get a community much farther off base than that.

Our values became as twisted as iron girders after a fire. Hollywood, Wall Street, Miami Beach, glamour girls, the Rose Bowl, the comic strips, a radio diet of soft soap, laxatives, pep talks and jazz—all conspired to keep millions of us insulated from reality for many hours in the day. Discipline is impossible in dream worlds. We lost our sense of discipline and of responsibility.

We were not soft and indolent, as is alleged. A nation is not soft which drives at 60 m.p.h.; and murders 40,000 citizens on the roads a year. We had just lost our way. We had forgotten what life was all about. We were perverting our deepest instincts—the relation of man to his environment and to the community. Each of us, God help us, in those dreadful years, was trying to see how far he could go in wrecking the community about him, in tearing apart the bonds which yoked him to his fellows, in gnawing at the hands which held him up.

Our job in 1942 is not to out-talk the enemy. Our job is to outshoot him. We are up against two-ton bombs, fifty-ton tanks and sixteen-inch shells. There is no publicity man in heaven, earth or hell who can tell us how to sell our way through them. We are being drawn back relentlessly to our foundations.

I repeat, it is about time.

3 ★ Benefits of War

Many who subscribed to the doctrine of the benefits of war conceded that "war is hell," but contended that "the constructive forces at work today . . . will be productive of widespread benefit and welfare." Democratic Representative John W. Flannagan, Jr., of Virginia, was typical of those who interpreted the war as a conflict between good and evil, and thought that war would unify the nation. He made the following remarks on December 16, 1941. [Congressional Record, 77th Cong., 1st Sess., LXXXVII, Part 14, A5608-9.]

Yes, my colleagues, this war had to come.

It is a war of purification in which the forces of Christian peace and freedom and justice and decency and morality are arrayed against the evil pagan forces of strife, injustice, treachery, immorality, and slavery. . . .

I do not know what happened at Pearl Harbor. It looks like we were asleep. I shudder when I think that some day I will be informed, in detail, of that gruesome spectacle brought about by the treacherous winged vultures of hell. From the fragmentary accounts we pick up we evidently sustained a severe loss in armament and paid an appalling price in dead and wounded.

But by reason of Pearl Harbor, I do know what happened in America. Some unknown power, in some secret, mysterious way, in the twinkle of an eye, transmitted to our inmost consciences the fearfulness of that treacherous disaster and the seriousness of the challenge confronting us, and our very souls became so inflamed with righteous wrath, so fired with patriotism, that our differences and divisions and hates melted into a unity never before witnessed in this country.

That unity, my colleagues, is so fixed, so firm, so cemented, that it is capable, not only of avenging Pearl Harbor, but a thousand Pearl Harbors.

Oh, no doubt there are those who will think I should not say it— I only give expression to my innermost thoughts when I do—but probably we needed a Pearl Harbor—a Golgotha—to arouse us from our self-sufficient complacency, to make us rise above greed and hate, to awaken us to a realization of our spiritual duties and responsibilities, and unite us in defense of the God-given ideals of liberty, freedom, and equality, of peace, justice, decency, and morality, upon which this Republic rests.

EXHORTATIONS TO SELF-SACRIFICE

Strenuous efforts were made to make Americans take part in war projects. Those responsible for civilian defense asserted that modern war meant "total danger, total sacrifice, total effort" and asked each citizen to contribute, in the words of Fiorello H. La Guardia, "an hour a day for the U.S.A." This might be done by enlisting in programs that ranged from training as air raid wardens to growing victory gardens, from serving as fire watchers to salvaging tin cans. The Office of Civilian Defense, after some false starts, provided an outlet for the energies of millions who wished to volunteer their services. Nevertheless, some voiced complaints that Americans regarded their part in the war too lightly, and the maintenance of morale became more difficult as the first wave of enthusiasm passed and the danger of actual attack grew more remote.

4 ★ "Volunteers in Offense"

On March 13, 1942 the New York State Council of Defense sent the following memorandum to chairmen of local civilian defense units. It described how individuals might assist the war effort and provided a justification for such participation. [New York State Council of War Papers, Collection of Regional History, Cornell University.]

Civilians in this war must be as fully prepared as our army, navy, or air force.

This war is diabolically different from all other wars. The pattern of axis aggression reaches down into the homes of the countries that have been attacked—destroying them, reducing them to rubble, searing them with flame. The helpless population suffer the brunt of the battle. It isn't a case of army against army, navy against navy, according to all former rules of war. This is a civilians' war—and as civilians we must face the full fury of our enemies, who have no respect for an "open city" nor an unarmed opponent.

Therefore, as civilians, we must prepare. We can divide that preparation of our civilian population into two broad areas—volunteer participation in civilian protection and volunteer participation in community services.

By "civilian protection" we mean the activities which aim at the protection of life and property. Under this heading come air raid precaution, auxiliary fire fighters, auxiliary police, rescue squads, demolition squads, emergency medical services—all of the services that go into action if disaster comes, whether from direct enemy action or from sabotage. These services must have absolute priority.

Civilians make good airplane spotters, communications workers, ambulance drivers. We need volunteers with physical stamina for these jobs—strong, loyal citizens. Both men and women can serve in the civilian protection forces organized under local city or county defense councils, in accordance with standards set by the State Defense Council.

Volunteer services in fields other than civilian protection fall into three broad areas. They represent the efforts of our citizens to increase the well-being, the morale of our home front, and thereby aid in winning the war.

FIRST: *In the home.* In each home we want to have persons trained in five forms of volunteer service: a first aider, a home nurse, a nutritionist, a family budget manager who has learned how to stretch the family dollar, and finally someone who knows how to take the best care of the family.

SECOND: *In the neighborhood.* We must learn to know our neighbors and to work together in our immediate neighborhoods to contribute what we can toward winning the war. The Division of Volunteer Participation will shortly have ready a ten-meeting series for neighborhood discussion groups, entitled "Fighting the War at Home." Its purpose is to bring us together in small neighborhood groups to discuss, to inform ourselves about blackout technique, fire-fighting, emergency medical care, budgeting, waste collecting, defense savings, victory gardens, and child care. A number of these discussion meetings will lead to definite courses which can be undertaken by those who are interested.

THIRD: *In the community.* There are many opportunities for those who live in villages or towns, to aid in the community's health and welfare activities. In the field of health, they can assist the public health nurses, serve as nurses' aides in hospitals, serve in child care and maternity clinics, offer to be blood donors. In the educational field there are opportunities for volunteers to assist in the instruction of aliens in language and citizenship; to act as aides in child development centers and day nurseries: aid in forming Youth Service Councils: aid in home economics training and in providing hot lunches for school children. In the welfare field we can offer ourselves to all types of public and private family welfare agencies.

This is the program of the New York State Defense Council. Are all parts being undertaken in your council? They must be, if we are to win the war.

5 ★ "What Can I Do?"

The following pamphlet, distributed by the Office of Civilian Defense, explained that even those citizens who did not volunteer for specific assignments had obligations, and suggested that self-denial might become a symbol of status. The cartoons illustrating the booklet bore such captions as: "Don't be an unwitting Nazi agent." [Office of Civilian Defense, Washington, 1942.]

War changes the pattern of our lives. It cannot change our *way of life,* unless we are beaten. The kids still play baseball in the corner lot— but they knock off early to weed the victory garden, cart scrap paper to the salvage center, carry home the groceries that used to be delivered. The factory whistle blows—but it calls three shifts of workers instead of one. The daily paper still has comics, but it's the front page that carries the answer to the urgent question "how are we doing?" All over America there's a new tempo, a new purpose, *a new spirit.*

Hard work isn't hard—it's a badge of courage. That "old clothes look" doesn't matter. It's smart to be mended. "Sorry m'am, we can't get any more of those." Good! That means materials are going where they belong—into war weapons.

Only one thing worries us.

"I'm too old to fight!"

"I'm too young to fight!"

"I'm busy all day cooking and cleaning and mending." . . .

But this is your war—and your part in it is clear. You don't need spare time. You need imagination to see the connection between tasks which to you may seem small and unimportant—and winning the war.

You need understanding, resourcefulness, self-discipline, determination, and love of America. . . .

Conservation is a war weapon in the hands of every man, woman, and child. And here are two simple rules for using your weapon:

1. *Get along with less*—Every time you decide *not* to buy something, you help to win the war. Be tough with yourself in making each decision. Luxuries are out, and lots of things we used to think of as necessities begin to look like luxuries as we get more and more war-minded.

2. Take good care of the things you have. Most of the comforts and conveniences you now enjoy will have to last you for the duration. It's only common sense to make them last as long as possible. But there is no need to become frantic about your possessions, or to attach too much importance to them. That kind of thinking leads to a wild scramble for possessions and then to hoarding. In wartime, hoarders are on the same level as spies; both help the enemy.

War production goes faster when home life runs smoothly, and so it is a good idea to keep our homes and personal possessions in good order and repair. Do it now—don't wait until your things are past repairing. The more shipshape and tidy we keep our homes and personal possessions the less we will feel the need to buy new things.

Most people understand the *why* of conservation, but they want to know *how*—how to get on without, how to use less so as to contribute to the war supply, how to save, substitute, and salvage. Here are some of the "hows."

Consider, for example, a material so scarce that civilians will not get any more of it for the duration—rubber. Rubber is high up on the list of things we must contribute to the war.

We have been slow in changing our driving habits. Toll-bridge receipts were higher in January 1942 than in January 1941. This news must have pleased Hitler. It is bad news for Americans—as bad as losing a battle.

We are beginning to do much better. Pleasure riding is out for the duration. As of today we must pool our cars for necessary use, for driving to work, to school, to the shops. We must share necessary rides with our friends and neighbors so that no car goes on the road with even one empty seat. The empty seat is a gift to Hitler. . . .

Make a thorough search of your closets, attic, cellar, and garage. You will be surprised at the amount of useless metal, rubber, rags, and paper that can be salvaged. Have a special place to put each kind of salvaged material. The children can help. . . .

V-Homes

Millions of Americans are fighting this war in their homes every day in the week, every week in the year. They are doing millions of hard jobs, full chores, making millions of small sacrifices. They are saving and salvaging, conserving and converting. They are foregoing small pleasures, putting up with inconveniences and annoyances. They are doing these things freely and gladly because they understand the meaning of their fight for freedom: freedom for themselves, their children, and the America they love.

These steadfast and devoted people receive no medals, no citations. They do not ask for recognition, but they deserve it, not only in justice to them, but as an incentive to go on working for victory. The road is long and hard, and all of us need cheer and encouragement.

The V-Home award is a badge of honor for those families which have made themselves into a fighting unit on the home front. If you and your family have earned such an award, you are entitled to put the V-Home certificate in your window. You will receive the award from your local Defense Council. If you and your family have not yet enlisted on the home front you can join today—the greatest civilian army in American history.

The V-Home certificate means something: it has to be earned. This is what it says:

THIS IS A V-HOME!

We in this home are fighting. We know this war will be easy to lose and hard to win. We mean to win it. Therefore we solemnly pledge all our energies and all our resources to fight for freedom and against fascism. We serve notice to all that we are personally carrying the fight to the enemy, in these ways:

I. *This home follows the instructions of its air-raid warden,* in order to protect itself against attack by air.

II. This home *conserves* food, clothing, transportation, and health, in order to hasten an unceasing flow of war materials to our men at the front.

III. This home *salvages* essential materials, in order that they may be converted to immediate war uses.

IV. This home *refuses to spread rumors* designed to divide our Nation.

V. This home *buys* War Savings Stamps and Bonds *regularly*.

We are doing these things because we know we must *to Win This War*.

6 ★ "Town Meetings for War"

In April, 1942, town meetings were held in various places as a testament to American unity. Supposedly spontaneous, they were in reality inspired by the Office of Civilian Defense, which arranged for widespread publicity. Although one OCD official feared that "local political, service, fraternal or other groups" would try to steal control of the affairs from local defense councils, the meetings seem to have come off satisfactorily. The following memorandum, sent by OCD Director James M. Landis to President Roosevelt on April 27, 1942, described the first of these "Town Meetings for War." [Franklin D. Roosevelt Papers, Official File 4422.]

The first four "Town Meetings for War" on Saturday were more successful than we had hoped in their basic objective—that of awakening all the elements of the community to their responsibilities for total participation for Victory.

In Northport, Alabama, 2000 of the town's 2500 population attended the meeting.

In Ontario, California, 3000 of the townspeople attended.

In Hannibal, Missouri, 4000 jammed the armory and 15,000 more lined the streets.

In Amenia, New York, the smallest of the communities, 500 towns-people and farmers from the countryside were present.

All meetings heard reports from their local defense officials on the war programs for their communities. There was little oratorical speech-making—simply short sincere tough talks. The people liked the idea and asked for more meetings.

There were opening and closing prayers; war mothers and the families of local war heroes were honored; war production and war bonds were high on the program; there were bands and the group sing-ing of the national anthem and the good old songs.

Whites and negroes [sic], old Americans and new Americans with traces of their homeland accents, the [American] Legion, the chambers of Commerce, the Red Cross, Boy Scouts, the farmers and the workers in the war plants—all these and many more groups participated actively. In short, these "Town Meetings for War" were all-American.

Each meeting was covered by sound newsreel and by *Life* maga-zine. Wire services and the local and regional press were highly inter-ested. Radio covered all meetings regionally.

SUSTAINING NATIONAL MORALE

The communications industry came to play a central part in the effort to marshal public sentiment. A Treasury Department radio program entitled "Millions for Defense" stimulated the sale of war bonds, and such popular shows as "Fibber McGee and Molly" incorporated messages on the need for nurses' aides. Motion pictures, according to Will H. Hays, "created a community of feeling throughout the civilian population that was one of the most powerful bulwarks of morale and incentives to sacrifice." Movie pro-ducers and radio broadcasters, who conceived their task to be one of inspiration as well as entertainment, recognized that people could be bound together by common hatred of the enemy no less than by the affirmation of American ideals.

7 ★ "Wilson"

Motion picture producer Darryl F. Zanuck, convinced that World War II had its origins in the frustration of Woodrow Wilson's peace proposals of 1919, suggested that the government make a documentary film on Wilson's life "to show the mistakes of the past so they could be avoided in the future." When the proposal was rejected, Zanuck himself produced the movie, although not as a strict documentary. With a screenplay by Lamar Trotti and with Alexander Knox in the title role, "Wilson" was a great success. Although they meant to use the past as a guide to the present, the film revealed how the war helped reshape Americans' conception of their history. [John Gassner and Dudley Nichols, eds., *Best Film Plays of 1943-1944* (New York: Crown Publishers, Inc., 1945). Reprinted by permission of Darryl F. Zanuck and 20th Century Fox Film Corporation.]

LANSING. Mr. President.

VON BERNSTORFF. Mr. President.

WILSON. Mr. Lansing. Your Excellency. (*Puzzled*) What is it, gentlemen?

LANSING (*greatly agitated*). Mr. President, I'm sorry to disturb you at such an hour, but Count von Bernstorff has just handed me another note from his government.

WILSON. Yes?

LANSING. Beginning *tomorrow*, Germany will resume its policy of unrestricted submarine warfare—

VON BERNSTORFF (*hastily*). We have no other choice, Mr. President.

LANSING.—and will sink on sight—and without warning—any neutral vessel entering European waters.

[*Wilson stares at von Bernstorff, hardly able to believe his ears.*]

VON BERNSTORFF. With certain exceptions, of course.

LANSING (*irony in his voice*). Yes, I believe one American ship will be permitted to sail from a designated port each week—provided it is properly lighted and marked.

[*Wilson continues to stare at von Bernstorff incredulously. The latter is obviously ill at ease.*]

VON BERNSTORFF. We deeply regret the necessity of this decision, Mr. President, and we sincerely hope you will not permit it to interfere with your noble efforts to bring about peace with our enemies.

WILSON (*coldly*). Sit down, sir! (*Von Bernstorff drops into a chair.*)

LANSING. We also have received indisputable proof within the last hour that the German Government has been using our own State Department cables in an effort to foment trouble between this country and Mexico.

WILSON (*white with anger*). What?

LANSING. With California, New Mexico, and parts of Texas as bait.

VON BERNSTORFF (*with a flash of Prussian anger*). I deny any such thing, Mr. President!

LANSING. The proof is overwhelming, Mr. President. There can be no doubt.

[*Von Bernstorff has visibly paled. He clutches the knob of his walking stick to keep his hands from shaking. Wilson looks at him and for a moment one thinks he might even attack the German agent. . . . Then he begins to speak—quietly at first, but with mounting passion as he goes on.*]

WILSON. Count von Bernstorff, for more than two years this Government has exercised every restraint in its efforts to remain neutral in this conflict. But you and your military masters apparently are determined to deny us that right.

VON BERNSTORFF. But I assure you, sir—

WILSON (*ignoring the interruption*). Every way we turn we run into a blank wall of German cruelty and stupidity. Every time we think we've escaped, you blindly—and *deliberately*—block us with some new outrage!

VON BERNSTORFF (*rising—full of German indignation*). Mr. President! . . .

WILSON. Sit down. Won't you Germans ever be civilized? Won't you ever learn to keep your word? Or to regard other peoples as men, women and children of flesh and blood and not as inferiors to be treated as you see fit—all in the name of your discredited German Kultur and race superiority?

VON BERNSTORFF (*again rising*). I wish to withdraw, Mr. President. . . .

WILSON. We are not exactly fools. We know about the spies and conspirators you've sent amongst us in an effort to corrupt our opinions through lies and rumors, and of your ceaseless attempts to sabotage our industries and commerce. (*Waving aside an interruption*) Unfortunately, some of our own people have fallen in with your plans, and day after day I see them going up and down this country doing your work, cry-ing out in their innocence that this is "just another European war" which can't touch America—building up false illusions of safety and security—appealing to our ancient traditions of isolation—while you smile behind their backs and go right ahead with your evil plans of world conquest and exploitation.

VON BERNSTORFF (*again rising*). I bid you good night, Mr. President.

WILSON. You will wait until I have concluded, Count von Bernstorff. (*As von Bernstorff sinks down again*) Is your Kaiser so contemptuous of American military prowess? Does he think we're so weak and disunited—just because we prefer peace to war—that we will not fight in any circumstances? Or is he so drunk with power that he can't understand that such action will unite this nation as never before in its history —and that he has made it clear at *last* that this is, in truth, a fight for freedom and decency against the most evil and autocratic power the world has ever seen? (*Turning to Lansing*) Mr. Lansing, you will hand His Excellency, Count von Bernstorff, his passports immediately. (*To von Bernstorff*) Good night, sir!

[*Count von Bernstorff gets to his feet and clicks his heels, speechless before the wrath of the President. Then he turns and marches out of the room, followed by Lansing, who bows to the President before he exits. Wilson stands looking after them for a moment in deep thought, and the scene draws in to afford a close view revealing the struggle and sense of outrage which von Bernstorff's announcement has produced. Slowly he turns and crosses and stands in front of the great, dimly-lit portrait of Washington, the scene moving with him, as we hear faintly the strains of "Yankee Doodle."*]

8 ★ Norman Corwin, "We Hold These Truths"

Written at the invitation of the U.S. Office of Facts and Figures, Norman Corwin's play was broadcast on December 15, 1941 to a radio audience of 60 million people. After describing how the Bill of Rights was added to the Constitution at the insistence of "the farmers and the clerks, the hackmen and the artisans, the grease-grimed blacksmiths in their shops," with the support of such prominent men as "Tom Jefferson, George Mason, Jimmy Madison, Pat Henry," the drama concluded with an inquiry into the contemporary relevance of the liberties obtained in 1791. [From More By Corwin *by Norman Corwin. Copy-*

right 1944 by Norman Corwin. Reprinted by permission of Holt, Rinehart & Winston, Inc.]

CITIZEN. A promise is a promise.

Has America's been kept? Has it come through peace and war and peace and war untarnished and unbroken?

Has it worked and is it working?

For the people, by the people? Is it going anywhere from here?

Are the rights the right rights? Are they rolling, do they function, do they click?

Who knows the answer better than the people? Whom better can we ask than the great custodians themselves, the hundred million keepers of the promise?

We shall ask them. Ask a few of them who stand for many more than few—the high and low among them.

Music: Theme Y out.

CITIZEN. Ladies and gentlemen, an office clerk.

CLERK. Well—(*clears throat*) we know what freedom is now. Looked for a while there like a lot of us'd forgot what it really meant and how much we had of it, but the news from the four corners of the earth reminded us, all right.

CITIZEN. Ladies and gentlemen, an editor.

EDITOR. There have been attacks on the freedom of the press and strangleholds of various sorts, but they've been broken every time; and today a man is free to start a paper, run it as he pleases, differ from the next man all he wants. That would make it seem to me, for one, that our rights have come down undamaged.

CITIZEN. Ladies and gentlemen, a worshiper.

WOMAN. I go to the church of my choice. And sometimes when I don't wish to go, I don't go.

CITIZEN. Ladies and gentlemen, an auto worker.

WORKER. We got the right to organize. We got the right to bargain collectively. Those are good rights, and we're proud of them, and we're better workers on account of them.

CITIZEN. Ladies and gentlemen, a manufacturer.

MANUFACTURER. There is nothing in any law which forbids us to forget class differences and work together to strengthen the sinews of our country.

CITIZEN. Ladies and gentlemen, an Okie.

OKIE. I got a right, ef'n I'm hongry an' out of work, which I is been, to go lookin' for work anywhere in my country. The big court says nobody cain't stop me from lookin'—dang it, that's my right.

CITIZEN. Ladies and gentlemen, a mother.

MOTHER. I might be afraid to bring a child into the world—but not to bring a citizen into the population of this country.

Music: Theme Y returns and sustains behind:

CITIZEN. From men beneath the rocking spars of fishing boats in Gloucester, from the vast tenancy of busy cities roaring with the million mingled sounds of work, from towns spread thinly through the Appalachians, from the assembly lines, the forges spitting flame, the night shifts in the mines, the great flat counties of the prairie States, from the grocers and from salesmen and the tugboat pilots and the motor-makers—affirmation! Yes! United proudly in a solemn day! Knit more strongly than we were a hundred fifty years ago!

Can it be progress if our Bill of Rights is stronger now than when it was conceived? Is that not what you'd call wearing well? The incubation of invincibility?

Is not our Bill of Rights more cherished now than ever? The blood more zealous to preserve it whole?

Americans shall answer. For they alone, they know the answer. The people of America: from east, from west, from north, from south.

Music: Theme Y concludes.

9 ★ Advertising the War Effort

War reversed the traditional themes of advertising: people were urged to do with less, not acquire more. The government popularized the slogan, "Use it up, wear it out, make it do or do without." In a book describing life on the home front for returning servicemen, Raymond Rubicam, head of a prominent advertising firm, offered this account of wartime hucksterism. [Raymond Rubicam, "Advertising," in Jack Goodman, ed., *While You Were Gone* (New York: Simon and Schuster, Inc., 1946), pp. 437-439. Copyright, 1946, by Simon and Schuster, Inc. Reprinted by permission of the publishers.]

At the opening of War Bond drives, as many as a thousand maga-
zines would run War Bond pictures or feature material on their covers;
often, in entire editions of newspapers every advertisement in the issue
would be devoted to War Bonds; and radio coverage would be on a
comparable scale. Supplementary media of every type supported the
effort. Even wrappers on diapers were pressed into service to advertise
War Bonds. Messages on the importance of bond buying were published
from the President, Stalin, Churchill, and all the leading generals and
admirals of the American armed services. Radio and motion-picture stars
originated or were furnished with ingenious and colorful ways of bringing their talents to bear.

Slogans like "Back the attack with War Bonds" and "You've done
your bit, now do your best!" were rallying forces for the drives.

Altogether, advertising space and time estimated to be worth $400,-
000,000 was donated to War Bond campaigns alone, and the number of
individual ads ran into the millions.

There were many brilliant advertisements which made telling emotional appeals for war support all along the line. One powerful example
of this type showed three young girls lined up along the wall in a Nazi
headquarters with a bullet-headed Nazi official leering at them. The headline of the advertisement was: "A high honor for your daughter," and
the text then said that if the Nazis win the war "You they may cast aside
and put to some ignominious task, such as scrubbing the sidewalks or
sweeping the streets. But your daughter . . . well, if she's young and
healthy and strong, a Gauleiter with an eye for beauty may decide she is a
perfect specimen for one of their experimental camps. A high honor for
your daughter."

Another dramatic page in the same series pictured a hangman's
noose with a smaller picture in the background of five people hanging.
The headline was: "Try this for size." "This type of collar," said the
text, "is designed for conquered people. . . . It's not a minute too soon
to get the picture straight . . . not a minute too soon to pitch in and
help turn the tide . . . not a minute too soon to do everything humanly
possible, now, to save our necks."

Another advertisement showed a civilian in his shirt sleeves asleep
on his living-room couch. "Are you comfortable, brother?" asked the
headline. And then the text went on to say, "That's good, brother. Just
sleep right through this war. Let some other guy do your share! What's
it to you that a kid just got bumped off in the Solomons . . . because
you couldn't be bothered with scrap collection? Sure, you out-smarted

the ration board on gas all right . . . and kept a certain Army plane in Africa out of the air. You're exhausted thinking up reasons why *not* to buy War Bonds . . . while thousands of American boys are going without food and sleep to protect your hide. Come on, get up off that fat can of yours . . . stop riding and start pushing! If this doesn't apply to you, tear it out and send it to someone it does!"

Perhaps the most widely quoted single advertisement of the war was one entitled "The Kid in Upper 4." While the specific job of this advertisement was to explain the problem of the railroads in handling both military and civilian travel, the advertisement had an appeal far beyond this. It told of a youthful soldier traveling away from home and shipping overseas. "Wide awake . . . listening . . . staring into the blackness," the kid reminisced about "the taste of hamburgers and pop . . . the feel of driving a roadster over a six-lane highway . . . a dog named Shucks, or Spot, or Barnacle Bill," and of the family left behind him. "There's a lump in his throat," the advertisement said, "and maybe a tear fills his eye. It doesn't matter, Kid. Nobody will see . . . it's too dark. . . ." Then to the public came this closing message: "Next time you are on the train, remember the kid in Upper 4. If you have to stand en route . . . If there is no berth for you . . . If you have to wait for a seat in the diner . . ." it is so that he may do his job. "To treat him as our most honored guest is the least we can do to pay a mighty debt of gratitude."

2 The War Economy

THE ROLE OF GOVERNMENT

During World War II, the government imposed comprehensive controls upon the economy. Although the Administration drew upon previous experience with industrial mobilization, the degree of intervention exceeded that of either World War I or the New Deal. Rationing prescribed what the housewife might buy; rent control governed what the landlord might charge; priorities determined what the manufacturer might produce. Industrial wages and agricultural prices were also regulated. These controls were tolerated because they were understood to be of a temporary nature and allowed for substantial economic improvement; even so, various groups which chafed under the restraints sought exemption in order to improve their status. Although many controls were lifted in 1945, the war had a lasting impact upon the nation's economic structure: it brought about a fairer distribution of income, a greater degree of industrial concentration, a consolidation of trade union strength, and far-reaching changes in the pattern of agricultural life.

10 ★ Edwin E. Witte, "What the War Is Doing to Us"

Early in 1943, Edwin E. Witte described the way in which federal intervention had produced a "mixed" economy, and compared the existing regulation with what had occurred under Woodrow Wilson. Witte, a leader in Wisconsin's efforts to improve industrial conditions, had helped draft the Social Security Act of 1935 and served for a time as a public member of the National War Labor Board. [The Review of Politics, V (January 1943), 3-25. Reprinted by permission.]

Most people will agree that the most important change wrought by the war has been the greatly increased participation of Government in our economic life. Government has always had a role in our economy, and the degree of its participation in economic life has been increasing for more than fifty years. The long time trend in this direction was greatly accelerated in the depression period. But Government is now participating in economic life to a degree never before known in this country and only remotely approached in the last war.

Of all of the changed relations which the war has brought between Government and business, none is probably more fundamental than the fact that the Government is now the purchaser of approximately one half of all the production of the American people. This percentage has been steadily increasing and is not yet at the maximum. The best gauge of the present situation is probably the extent of the Government expenditures in relation to the total national income. Our total production is now at a rate of approximately 10 billion dollars per month. The Government expenditures total 6 billion dollars, of which 5.5 billions are for war purposes. . . .

The relations of the Government to the half of our present economy devoted to war purposes are those of a monopolistic purchaser, but one so necessitous that costs are secondary. Most of the goods the Government buys are not purchased on the markets but are specially produced under contract. Of most of these goods, the Government is the only possible user; of others, it has pre-empted the entire supply; for still others it satisfies its demands before anyone else may buy. So great are the needs of the Government, however, that in many lines it must utilize all possible sources, no matter how costly the production may be. The Government buys not only from the efficient but the inefficient and even the submarginal. The price it must pay is of secondary consideration; winning the war and maximum production of the goods and services which will contribute to that end is the all important objective of economic policy.

The situation in this part of our present economy is such that the normal price system has ceased to function. The last war produced a great outcry against cost-plus contracts. In this war there have been few cost-plus contracts on the model of World War I. But the Government in making its purchases has again had to come to a system of meeting the costs of every producer from whom it buys goods and services. Early in the defense effort the Government made its purchases on a competitive bid basis, which meant that it bought from the more efficient producers who could offer it the most favorable prices. Within a week after the Axis made its treacherous attack upon this country, we abandoned the system of purchases on bid. We substituted for it the negotiated contract, in which the Government makes a bargain with each producer without resort to competitive bidding. The more recent "renegotiation of contracts" does not fundamentally alter this practice, although it will result in lower prices in many instances. What is basic is that the Government pays different prices to different producers, in each case meeting their anticipated or actual costs, with a margin above cost sufficient to induce the desired production. It pays a higher price to the inefficient than the efficient because it needs all of the production it can get.

The Government also is exercising ever increasing control over the half of the economy in which it is not the purchaser of the goods and services produced. I need do no more than to call your attention to the variety of these controls. Some of them had their parallels in the last war, others represent complete innovations, and nearly all have gone beyond anything that was attempted in World War I. In that war we had numerous priorities: priorities for raw materials, for partially finished goods, for transportation, and, to a limited degree, for labor. In this war, we have a much larger number of priorities for materials. Entirely new controls to insure that the producers of the most essential war goods will have the materials which they need, however, are now making their appearance in the allocation system, under which the producers of the essential war goods not merely get priorities for the materials they need but an actual allotment of these materials.

In relation to transportation and communication we have thus far had fewer priorities, but many new controls necessitated by the peculiar problems confronting us in this war. The Government has not taken over the operation of the railroads, the telegraph lines, and the express companies, as it did in the last war. But the Office of Defense Transportation has required the pooling of facilities and placed restriction on the shipment of many commodities. It has required reduction in truck mileage, including milk and grocery deliveries and many other services. The speed at which private automobiles may be driven is now restricted by federal orders throughout the country and gasoline use has been limited, to save both rubber and transportation.

Restrictions upon labor, also, already are much more extensive than in the last war, although still in an early stage. In World War I, some states passed compulsory work laws; in the summer of 1918, Provost-General Crowder issued his famous "work or fight" order; in the last months of the war, war contractors were directed to hire all unskilled labor through the public employment offices (an order which never was really enforced). The authority conferred upon the War Manpower Commission to date goes beyond measures of this character. It permits the Manpower Commission to "freeze" labor in any industry and to control hiring by any employer. To date this power has been exercised sparingly. Orders have been issued "freezing" labor employed in non-ferrous metal mines, in lumbering in the western states, in dairy farming, in the federal service itself, and through the device of establishing a maximum hiring wage in the Detroit tool and die industry. Very probably these are merely the beginning, as it is only now that the labor supply situation is becoming critical.

There has been no law prohibiting strikes, but immediately after Pearl Harbor the leaders of organized labor, practically without exception, pledged that there would be no strikes in wartime. The National War Labor Board has been established to authoritatively settle all labor disputes not settled through collective bargaining and mediation. While there are no criminal penalties, the President through vigorously supporting the War Labor Board, has made its authority compulsory upon both employers and employees.

Controls of broad scope have also been applied to consumers. In the last war there was some rationing of materials and of a limited number of consumers' goods. Lumber and other building materials could not be used except for permitted construction. We rationed sugar and a small number of other commodities. In the last two months of the war, we had wheatless and meatless days on a voluntary appeal basis. In the present war, the number of rationed commodities is already much greater and many products are denied entirely to ordinary civilian users.

Price controls also are very much more extensive. In the New Deal period we made great efforts to increase prices, with the expressed objective of restoring the price level of 1926. In wartime, even before prices recently reached the 1926 level, we have introduced extensive price controls to keep down prices. The commodities for which maximum prices have been set embrace nearly all of the commodities in common use, including, under recent Congressional legislation, a large part of our agricultural production.

But the most important innovation in this respect is wage control. In the last war maximum wages were not prescribed in any industry. Today all wage increases are subject to governmental approval and strict limitations are placed upon the maximum increases that may be granted. We have even set a top limit to the salaries which may be paid to executives.

Most drastic of all the controls introduced, however, are the direct orders of Government prohibiting or limiting production, with the end in view of compelling the owners of plants in such industries and the workers therein to shift their production to war purposes. The nearest approach which we had to anything of this kind in the last war was our war-time Prohibition. It has now been forgotten but it was a fact, that nation-wide Prohibition came to this country not through the Eighteenth Amendment but through an order of President Wilson prohibiting the utilization of any grain for brewing or distillation. But while we closed the breweries and the distilleries, we did not, in the last war, tell them or any other producers what they must produce. In the present war not only has our pre-war greatest single manufacturing industry—automobiles—been told to stop production and to get into war work, but similar orders have been issued upon many other industries. In an even larger number of industries the Government has issued orders limiting the war-time production to a specified percentage of the peace-time output. Pressure has been brought upon such industries to concentrate production in a few plants in order that the other plants in the industry may become available for war production. Beyond this, we have now begun to limit production in many industries which cannot be converted to war uses, with the end in view of releasing labor to the war industries.

In the NRA days there was a great deal of talk about "industrial self-government." This slogan seems very far remote in the present war economy. We do not yet have a completely planned economy such as exists in Germany, Russia, and Japan, but new controls are being introduced daily. Large segments of our economy are little affected by the new governmental controls. Much free choice remains to producers. Aside from the men called to the colors, no one has yet been told exactly where he must work, and production for the Government is still a matter of contractual arrangement freely entered into by the producers. Government does not run businesses in every detail. Yet it is accurate to say that our economy is rapidly becoming a completely planned economy.

It is not, however, a socialistic economy in the Marxian sense. Private property remains predominant. The profit motive still has a large role in our economy. Individual initiative, work, and thrift count as much as ever, if not more. In the mixed public and private economy we have long had, war has resulted in greater emphasis upon the public elements, but ours is still a mixed economy, which is not accurately described as either capitalism or socialism, as these terms have been used by the theorists.

What we have witnessed to date is the development of many new relationships between Government and business. Approximately 80 per cent of all funds invested for the expansion of war industrial facilities have come from the Government. Far more frequently than in World War I, the Government has built plants and leased them for operation to private corporations, retaining title to the property. In other cases, the Government, through the Reconstruction Finance Corporation, has loaned the money needed for war expansion. In the emergency plant facilities contracts, the Government agrees to reimburse contractors in a 60 month period the entire cost of facilities acquired for war production purposes, the title to which remains with the private owners until fully paid for; and the Government will even supply all the money needed for the original purchases. In a very real sense the Government has gone into partnership with private business for an all-out war production effort. The Government supplies most, if not all, of the capital, buys the goods produced, and generally controls operations, but with the actual management in private hands. To complete the picture, the Government has largely relied upon industrialists, who have entered its employ or have been loaned to it as "dollar-a-year" men, for general direction of the war production effort. If this be socialism, it is certainly not the socialism of Marx or Lenin.

11 ★ *Franklin D. Roosevelt,* Curbing Inflation

The efforts of the Office of Price Administration to stabilize the cost of living in 1942 caused some dissatisfaction and led to congressional pressure to allow a measure of inflation. In July, OPA Director Leon Henderson warned the President that attempts were being made to cripple the stabilization program by limiting his agency's jurisdiction and curtailing its appropriations. On July 11, Roosevelt wrote to Vice-President Henry Wallace and Senators Alben Barkley and Carter Glass explaining the importance of effective price control. [Franklin D. Roosevelt Papers, Official File 4403.]

I am necessarily away for two or three days and therefore not able to keep in touch with the O.P.A. appropriation. However I greatly hope that it will come out of committee in such form as to sustain the whole purpose of holding down the cost of living in a practical way. For example if amendments are put on limiting this, that or the other price of this, that or the other commodity in this, that or the other State, we would start a very bad logrolling custom.

So also if we start in redetermining and republishing parity price data, especially on manufactured articles in which some parity product is used, we would face an administrative complexity which would cause so much delay that the actual cost of living would get out of hand.

The whole question comes down to the necessity for quick action and a firm hand in stopping the dreaded spiral from getting under way. Our whole war effort will be greatly influenced by this. So also the national debt at the end of the war will be much greater than otherwise. So also competition for special favors between business, agriculture and labor will be automatically increased.

I am deeply concerned and trust that our war effort will be enhanced and not crippled.

BUSINESS PROSPERITY

Soaring government expenditures in wartime helped bring about the business recovery that had eluded the New Deal. The statistics are startling: during the war, 17 million new jobs were created, industrial production increased by 96 per cent, and corporate profits after taxes more than doubled. Although war needs consumed about one-third of the output, expanded production ensured a reasonably adequate supply of consumers' goods. Prosperity was not the only product of war. It also led to the creation of a synthetic rubber industry, carried industrialization into new areas in the West and South, hastened a trend toward concentration in business, and prompted internal changes in corporate structure. Finally, the prestige that derived from participation in the war and a recognition that prosperity depended on government support encouraged a measure of business accommodation to the welfare state.

12 ★ Merlo J. Pusey, "Revolution at Home"

Although military requirements spurred a general upturn in the economy, they sometimes damaged small businessmen and certain regions. Some of the implications of industrial combination and geographic dispersal were evaluated by Merlo J. Pusey, a Washington journalist and author, in the summer of 1943. Pusey believed that the nation was "shaping a new future under the pressure of war." [South Atlantic

Quarterly, XLII (July 1943), 207-19. Reprinted by permission of the magazine and the author.]

. . . The narrow margin between operating costs and prices in some industries is storing up headaches for us in the reconstruction period. Perhaps it is also hastening the transformation of our economic system, for of course industry lives on profits. This "squeeze" is likely to deprive numerous war contractors of the capital they will need to reconvert their plants to peacetime production. Some are able to maintain a healthy financial position now because of the vast amount of equipment they are turning out. But there is no certainty in the manufacture of war supplies. Tank production, for example, was recently curtailed because scarce steel could be used to better advantage in escort vessels. Guns in great demand today may be obsolete tomorrow. Material shortages often force slowdown operations. If, in the face of these uncertainties and reconversion expenses, industry is pinched too severely between stationary prices and rising costs, it will have, as the Brookings Institution has pointed out, neither the funds nor the incentive to provide maximum employment at the end of the war. Incidentally the shortage of manpower, the ceilings on prices, and the almost miraculous new inventions and processes evolving under pressure of war are encouraging the use of labor-saving devices that will further complicate the problem of post-war employment.

Still more cataclysmic is the industrial "purge" that is being managed jointly by the Army and the War Production Board. While big industry, fed by government capital and war orders, is growing bigger every day, small industry is being wrecked by the withholding of priorities and materials. The problem is clearly stated by investigators for the Senate Committee on Education and Labor:

Throughout the first two and a half years of our effort one hundred of America's largest corporations have received 75 per cent of all war contracts by dollar volume. To them has gone the bulk of new plants built at Government expense, over fourteen billions of dollars. To them are flowing in increasing numbers the workers seeking jobs in war industry. America, a land of giant corporations before the war, will emerge from this war with a larger share of its vastly expanded economy controlled by a smaller number of firms.

This situation . . . has been accompanied by the destruction of one small community after another through the shutting down of its factories and the migration of its people. The face of America is already greatly changed. If we continue destroying America's small businesses and uprooting smaller communities, and many of our large ones as well, we shall not recognize postwar America.

Similar fears have been expressed by the Tolan Committee investigating migration and war problems for the House of Representatives. In spite of numerous campaigns to save little business, small concerns are giving up the ghost at an alarming rate. Many of them will never be revived. And this is only a beginning. Several industries have been required to simplify and standardize their products, and concentration of civilian industry in the most efficient plants may be undertaken before victory is won.

Anyone familiar with the extent of these changes in our business structure would be blind not to see that they may profoundly affect our way of life. For small business has been a sort of economic frontier. That is to say, it has offered alternative means of livelihood to millions of men and women without the capital to become large-scale manufacturers or merchants and without the temperament to punch time clocks and pay union dues. It has nursed the spirit of economic freedom and maintained some degree of competition with our behemoths of industry and trade. Little plants operating in their own way have thus tended to give balance, flexibility, and relief from tension to our entire economic system. They have been a bulwark of democracy as well as of social stability.

No deliberate squeeze was planned to rout little business. The armed forces were in a hurry to get the work of rearming America under way. In their rush to get orders on paper, they failed to divide the business equitably or reasonably among all usable plants. Nor did the WPB insist on widespread or systematic subcontracting with the smaller firms. In the circumstances it was inevitable that the giants of industry should claim all the scarce materials and leave little business with neither war work nor the wherewithal to carry on civilian pursuits. It is easy to understand this outcome and to absolve officials of ulterior motives. But small firms that are being crushed beneath the priorities system will be just as dead as if their liquidation had been decreed as a national policy.

Certain advantages will undoubtedly accrue from this new emphasis on bigness. In the housing industry, for example, inefficient contractors operating on a shoestring are being replaced by large companies building two hundred to a thousand dwelling units at one time. To keep under the $6,000 ceiling on private homes built for war workers and at the same time make a profit, large-scale operations become imperative. Modern building methods are employed out of necessity. More important, large companies are learning that there are big opportunities in building houses which wage earners can afford to rent or buy. Here we have the nucleus of what may become a vast postwar industry capable of immeasurably improving the environment in which millions of our people live. Perhaps this particular triumph of bigness seems welcome chiefly because we have never before had a housing industry in the modern sense of the word. In any event, it does not minimize the tragic connotations which the death cry of little business carries to the ears of a great democracy. . . .

Much thought had been given to the location of war plants in the days when there seemed to be time to think about such problems. But Hitler's sweeping conquests in Europe and Japan's attack on Pearl Harbor forced the conversion of existing heavy industry to war use and the construction of new plants wherever they could be most conveniently located at the moment. Long-range interests in the systematic distribution of industry quickly gave way to a clamor for more speed in fabricating weapons for ourselves and our allies.

So we have built an enormous portion of our vast war plant within close range of big industries where expert management and skilled labor were at hand. Baltimore, Indianapolis, Buffalo, Hartford, St. Louis, Detroit, Los Angeles, Portland, Seattle, and numerous other cities find their manufacturing plants expanding at a rate that seemed impossible in peacetime. Detroit has sucked into its voracious mills enough manpower to make a new city much larger than Denver. Its satellite cities— Flint, Saginaw, Lansing, and Jackson—appear to have duplicated that feat on a smaller scale.

Of course, the lightning of war did not strike all the big cities with equal intensity. New York is suffering from a wave of unemployment because its consumer-goods industries are not readily adjustable to the making of tanks, airplanes, or ammunition. The jewelry industry in Providence is quietly starving for metal. But at near-by Hartford, where typewriters have given way to pistols and machine-tool makers are enjoying their golden age, every foot of space and every ounce of energy is at a premium. War is pushing Hartford ahead as ruthlessly as it is shoving New York behind. . . .

One exception to the general trend stands out in striking contrast. That is the sudden spurt of industrialization in the West. Great Salt

Lake and Utah valleys, for example, are undergoing the most profound changes they have experienced since Brigham Young's pioneers broke their parched soil nearly a hundred years ago. Great military establishments have taken the place of quiet farms. Peaceful landscapes have given way to smoke-belching behemoths of industry. Aluminum, radio parts, coke, steel, and other strategic products are beginning to pour out of an area that has heretofore been noted chiefly for the exportation of Mormonism. . . .

Taken as a unit, the West is feeling the stimulus of war industry more keenly than either the North or the South. In 1940 the West had only 10.5 per cent of the country's population. But more than 13 per cent of the government's war-plant fund is being spent there, chiefly for permanent assets. One explanation is the pull of power. Southern California, the beneficiary of Boulder Dam power, has become a seething caldron of war industry. San Diego was until recently known as the "hottest spot" in the whole national picture of wartime dislocations. Los Angeles has eclipsed even the fantastic peacetime records of that city. The Golden State as a whole is getting more than $390,000,000 in Federal money for war plants. That gives it a sizable lead on the great industrial state of New York, and puts it far ahead of all New England in the wartime expansion of industrial capacity.

In the Northwest, Seattle is the hub of an amazing workshop for war. Grand Coulee and Bonneville dams are doing for the Northwest what Boulder Dam has done for Southern California and Nevada. Their great resources of power attract war industries as certainly as a bag of oats attracts a mule. The investment of Federal funds in war plants in the state of Washington will equal $80 per capita (1940 census). That outpouring of funds added to previous investments in power has given the Columbia River Valley and Puget Sound region great opportunity to raid neighboring states for manpower. And they are making the most of it. War has thus thrown into double-quick pace the industrial revolution that was already under way in the West.

The meaning of these social and economic upheavals is plain. "The hand that signs the war contract," as a Senate committee said recently, "is the hand that shapes the future." Metal-ribbed Nevada has acquired new government-financed plants costing the equivalent of nearly $600 for every resident. The agricultural Dakotas have no new war plants. In each case the consequences will be far-reaching. For in this nation-wide mobilization there is no chance to maintain the *status quo.* If strategy and geography do not thrust a community into the maelstrom of war activity, its resources will be drained into other areas where they can better serve the national interest. So the whole pattern of our economic and social life is undergoing kaleidoscopic changes, without so much as a bomb being dropped on our shores.

13 ★ *Eric Johnston,* "America Unlimited"

"Ring out defeatism, ring out lugubrious philosophies of maturity, satiety, and senility! Ring in faith and self-confidence!" So declared Eric Johnston, president of the Chamber of Commerce and spokesman for an important segment of the business community. A man whose own career seemed not unlike that of an Horatio Alger hero, Johnston ascribed his success to "the familiar American mixture of robust striving, bold risks, self assurance, and good luck." In advancing the notion of a "People's Capitalism," he revealed some of the changes in business attitudes bred by wartime conditions. [From *America Unlimited*, by Eric Johnston, pp. 22-3, 34-8, 55-8, 74-5, 93-7, 107, 113-16, 144-47. Copyright 1942, 1943, 1944 by Eric Johnston. Reprinted by permission of Doubleday & Company, Inc.]

Areas of Agreement

During the first ten years of Mr. Roosevelt's occupancy of the White House it saw exceedingly few callers who could speak up for management and finance. Those who did call were too prone to speak softly and pull their punches—perhaps they had been convinced by the anti-business orations that they were really criminals at heart. Many of the President's closest associates rarely overlooked an opportunity to throw the harpoons into private enterprise as a system and its individual exponents. The bad feeling was mutual, amounting to a feud.

One of my main hopes, when elected to head the Chamber of Commerce in May 1942, was to end that feud, to heal that breach. With the nation at war, the danger of a continued struggle between business and government was that much more apparent. The Chamber is the most representative business organization in the country, made up of 1,800 local chambers and trade associations, with an underlying membership of nearly a million businessmen, the vast majority in the small and medium-sized business categories. Its *rapprochement* with the Administration seemed to me a primary objective in the public interest. Business had every right to its criticisms of the government, and it had the duty of defending its views. But those things, it seemed to me, are not inconsistent with co-operation in the huge area of public well-being where business and government could work together. . . .

Franklin Roosevelt, it seems to me, is especially sensitive to the currents of public opinion. Like all highly capable political leaders, he has some of the attributes of a "medium," in that he feels and reacts to popular trends of emotion. His mellowed attitude toward business is a reflection of the fact that business is retrieving a large measure of the public confidence that it had enjoyed before the depression. . . .

Neither Right Nor Left

Certain doctrinaire radicals regard all economic life in terms of what Karl Marx called "class struggle." In other words, they look upon relations between capital and labor as a permanent conflict in which we can hope, at best, for an occasional armistice. This theory is also accepted, in effect if not in words, by extremists in the private capitalist camp who would deny the inherent rights of labor. Both extremes are guilty of absolutist thinking. In practice, agreement and co-operation between labor and capital in the interests of common goals have been more vital and more real than the class struggle.

The same fallacy of absolutist thinking muddies the waters of relations between business and government. Advocates of state domination of all economy of the sort who came to the fore in the New Deal period regard government as in permanent conflict with private enterprise. That assumes another variety of class war in which one or the other must go down in defeat. And again diehard partisans of the *laissez-faire* ideal in effect agree with them, since they, too, look upon business and government as engaged in a struggle to the death. One group wants private enterprise to come out triumphant in this tussle, the other wants the government to emerge as the total master. But the thinking underlying both attitudes is the same.

I believe that we must free ourselves from this black-and-white thinking. To conserve the constructive and useful values in capitalism we must not seek to freeze it. We must not hem it in by too many taboos and restrictions. Within the main pattern of individual freedom it must remain resilient, adaptable, and thus thoroughly alive. The threat against capitalism does not come from just one direction. It also comes from the opposite corner. Let us look at this double menace.

First, there are those ultra-conservatives who are alarmed by change, any sort of change, and hence would turn back the clock of history. They would block the inexorable forward march of labor unionism, and would restrict government to the more primitive role it played in a more primitive day and age. Whatever the views or the motives of such people, the plain fact is that they automatically place themselves in the camp of unreasoning reaction—which is quite a different thing from intelligent conservatism. I think that the impact of war, fortunately, is jolting some of these people out of their absolutist attitudes; they are becoming fewer in number and many of their leaders are being mellowed and tempered by experience.

Second, at the other end of the ideological scale are the clamorous collectivists. Psychologically these are one breed, whether they call themselves fascists, communists, socialists, or superplanners. . . .

Most of them may not agree among themselves. Each contributes a piece or two to the over-all picture of a planned and virtually automatic world. From cradle to grave, from womb to tomb, life would be charted in advance. What every man shall plant or manufacture, how much he shall use, systems of economic priorities and rationing, administered by state and national and finally international boards and agencies would be elaborated—and presumably enforced by police action. Where the collectivist schemes provide a role for private enterprise, as many of them do, the risk element is taken out, a fair return is guaranteed on investment, and markets are assured in advance.

Most of these collectivists are well-meaning and idealistic. They are so conscious of the unsavory by-products of the capitalist way of life that they are blind to its accomplishments and blinder still to its unexploited potentialities. In their annoyance they would throw out the baby with the bath water. Even the sorry record of physical degradation, moral bankruptcy, terror, and war in the countries which have tried collectivism and state dictatorship does not frighten these theorists. They find excuses and fool themselves into believing that the American version of the totalitarian life will be different, more palatable.

I am convinced that I speak for the great majority of Americans in insisting that there is a middle ground of reality somewhere between these extreme threats to our traditional life. Call us progressives, or liberal progressives, or conservative liberals—such tags have lost their old meanings in the present crisis of growth and change. Whatever the tag, we deny that America faces a choice between a congealed old order and some experimental new order. On the contrary, we feel that those who narrow down the choice between such repugnant extremes are dangerously confusing the issue.

We believe in the middle way: the way of realistic adjustment between old-style *laissez-faire* capitalism and current economy. We reject rule-of-thumb absolutist thinking from any political direction. . . .

We prosper best under the freedom of give-and-take. Americans will accept collective action through their government but only to achieve purposes which cannot be achieved by private capital. They ascribe no wonder-working talents to government. They will sacrifice no portion of their treasured individual freedoms to compensate for collective chores. They will use *all* the institutions at their disposal to get results, and that does not exclude government. The successors of the New Deal in office will not dump all the worth-while advances made in recent years. They will not because they cannot. New facts and new attitudes have come into existence. But they can and must revise the innovations where these block the flow of investment capital and otherwise tend to stall the capitalist mechanisms. . . .

Brought up on the Jeffersonian idea that the government is best which governs least, Americans will have no truck with the statist dictum that the government is best which governs most. But as practical men they recognize change and are ready to utilize government beyond the limits visualized in Jefferson's more primitive society.

In the same way they will have no truck with those who see the possibilities of economic life only as a contest between labor control and management control, as a perpetual seesaw of strikes, lockouts, struggles for dominance. They believe in arbitration and accommodation, and are convinced that empiric reason and cold logic must displace brute force in industrial relations. Their common sense and native shrewdness reject theories of automatic happiness and planned security, just as they would reject theories of perpetual motion. . . .

Quacks and Cure-alls

In defending capitalism I do not gloss over its deficiencies or applaud its unpretty by-products. I have no more use for the excrescences of the competitive enterprise system than the most ardent proponent of Utopia Now. I do not yield to any socialist or communist in deploring the conditions of the so-called submerged tenth or underprivileged third.

I share their sorrow, and often their shame, for the sharecroppers, the migrant workers, the slum dwellers, the "okies," the hillbillies, the ill-housed, and the undernourished.

If I could honestly agree with them that there is a short cut to perpetual plenty, freedom, and glory, I would join them. But I cannot agree to this proposition. Their Utopias, where they have been tried on a small scale in Brook Farm types of colonies, have always fizzled out in conflict and bankruptcy. But at best the scale is everything; what may be possible in a small, sheltered group, artificially selected and protected, turns to gibberish in a great and complex nation.

Too frequently, I have observed, a pathological hatred for those who are well off—a kind of blind fury against success as such—plays a larger role in the thinking of political Utopians than concern for the poor and the suffering. That is why they seem content when "upper classes" are "liquidated," even if the other classes are thereby sunk more deeply into want and political oppression.

The more extreme critics of capitalism decry its materialism, its emphasis on production, wealth, the gadgets of comfort. Actually, however, they are the ones who carry materialism to its ultimate, in that they are willing to barter freedom for economic security. As the price for minimal economic safety, for bread and a roof, they seem prepared to submit unquestioningly to a total Authority, the state, and to relinquish that freedom of action and that freedom of conscience for which most men are content to accept economic hazards.

I belong to those spokesmen for the capitalist order who accept it enthusiastically *despite* its shortcomings. We accept the steel *despite* the slag. We accept the beauty and grandeur of man's life on earth *despite* unavoidable diseases, disasters, inevitable death. We are convinced that capitalism is the system that has yielded more desirable results than any actually tried by man. We not only wish to remove attendant evils and injustices, but believe that capitalist economy itself provides the best and surest and fastest means of accomplishing these purposes. . . .

The question, therefore, is whether we compare life under a capitalist dispensation with some abstract dream of arcadian bliss, or with reality under other economic and political systems, past and present. One need not ignore or approve existing evils to recognize that capitalism has released human energy beyond any system of life in the past; that it has spread the products of that energy to a greater number than ever before in history; that it has "unfrozen" society, enabling men to rise, regardless of birth and race and class, as never before; and, above all, that it has brought more genuine liberty and dignity and self-respect to the masses of mankind than any other known order of living.

These are the achievements we are asked to forget, the system we are urged to scrap, by the extremists, whether quacks or honest crackpots. . . .

The New Deal Appraised

By this time there are few socially minded American leaders who deny that many of the reforms initiated by the New Deal had been long overdue. The more candid among them will acknowledge that many of the changes would have been put into effect by any other administration. They were "in the cards." Only the hectic prosperity of the pre-New Deal years and the smugness it had induced postponed legislation and recognition of society's obligations to its citizenry that were inevitable in any case.

The main evil of the New Deal period, as I have already intimated, was its spirit of vendetta and class warfare—its refusal to explore and exploit areas of agreement. Mr. Roosevelt and most of his lieutenants took their stance on the heaving margins of difference and mutual suspicions. It was that which made their aim erratic and surrounded their every act—including the most laudable and sensible—with a feverish atmosphere of crusading, do-or-die warfare.

The New Dealers were not alone to blame for this ugly situation. It takes at least two to make a quarrel, and many of the "antis" happen to be as gifted and as passionate in making quarrels as Mr. Roosevelt himself, which is saying a great deal. Our very traditions of free speech and uninhibited mudslinging served as guarantees that the fracas would be loud and lively—and it has been. The business-baiters and the Roosevelt-haters proved equally lusty fellows. The American, as Hitler and Tojo are discovering, is a mighty scrapper, whether in foreign or domestic conflicts. . . .

A People's Capitalism

I see three main capitalisms in the world.

There is the capitalism of the bureaucrats. I am against it in its extreme forms in the totalitarian countries. I am against it in its seedling growths in our own country.

Second, there is the capitalism of private monopoly and special privilege. I am against it wherever it seeks to control and to dominate. The fact that it is private gives us at least this advantage over state capitalism: the power of government can be used to curb its activities. But though it is private it is not private *enterprise*, since it prevents the unhampered flow of enterprise capital in a freely competitive market.

Finally, there is what I venture to call a people's capitalism. I come from it. I want to see it survive for every poor boy and girl in America after me. Not only survive, but triumph. I am especially concerned with its survival because only America, I believe, can light the world toward an ultimate capitalism of everybody—a capitalism that is bound neither by government domination nor by private monopoly domination.

The essence of the capitalism of the bureaucrats, in the lands of the superstates, is that officials take the people's money and with it make themselves the only investing and managing capitalists. Thus every Russian business unit is owned by the state but also pays taxes to the state. These taxes are so high, and the administrative costs are so high, that they often double or even quadruple the prices on goods to the consumer. From taxes and profits the government obtains new capital which is invested in new business exactly as the bureaucrats please. . . .

When the domination is exercised by a few private companies and individuals, it is no sweeter. I am equally opposed to a capitalism that permits domination by private firms or corporations already established. This brand of monopolistic capitalism has long been gaining ground in some parts of Europe, especially in Britain. In America it has been under a legal ban since the Sherman Anti-trust Law was enacted in 1890.

Monopoly practices persist despite the law, just as other illegal practices in other areas of national life persist. Our court records provide indubitable proofs of the efforts of monopolistic business to suppress free enterprise in our free country. I believe that defenders of the capitalist system who close their eyes to such realities are defeating their own objectives. They are, in effect, offering the American people private domination in place of state domination, and are in truth enemies of private enterprise. The London *Economist*, referring to monopoly capitalist practices, calls them "a conspiracy of the inefficient."

I am not speaking against bigness. Some of the largest of our business organizations are the most democratic in their economic methods. They practice open competition and leave their respective industries open to all. Indeed, they often prosper by reason of this competition, which keeps them on the alert and prevents their bureaucratization. . . .

There is only one capitalism that is proof against bureaucratic domination: A people's capitalism. It is the capitalism that requires a population with savings—capital—in their pockets; business opportunities wide open to all who wish to enter with their savings, even on the smallest scale; honest and unimpeded competition to bring prices lower, in order to increase the purchasing power, the savings, and the capital of the people.

A people's capitalism is what America has prospered on, though monopolistic interference has occasionally barred its path. A people's capitalism puts the total people first. It goes beyond the dictum "What's good for business is good for *you*." It knows an even better one: "What's good for the people is good for *business*."

A people's capitalism is various, flexible, highly adaptable. It is the essence of what we have called earlier the Middle Way. The only absolute it accepts is freedom. Within the frontiers of that absolute all things are relative, living, adjustable. It has room for businesses from the smallest to the largest, for co-operative enterprise on the part of farmers, small producers in industry, and consumers.

A people's capitalism such as I am describing may not be what some spokesmen of business have in mind, but it is what the average American has in mind when he speaks of free economy. It is the kind of capitalism equally distasteful to the statist, the super-planner, the socialist, and communist on one side, and the monopolist, the cartel builder, the financial imperialist on the other.

A people's capitalism, as I see it, welcomes unsubsidized co-operative agricultural societies which legitimately serve to protect adequate incomes for farmers. It welcomes labor unions which legitimately strive to protect adequate incomes for wage earners. It welcomes professional organizations, business and trade associations, or any other type of free and autonomous organization. . . .

The theory and practice of a people's capitalism are summed up in the idea that the broadest road toward more jobs is more job creators. In achieving its purposes it does not reject the help of government. There has never been a "neutral" government. Every government, by the things it does and the things it refrains from doing, helps *some* capitalism. Our own government has at times aided monopolistic capitalism and at other times bureaucratic capitalism. It can and should be encouraged to throw its weight on the side of the people's capitalism. . . .

Our Contribution to Victory

Government necessarily assumed broad authority and has played a dominant part in the war production direction. It has had to control the flow of materials and exercise other economic powers which normally belong to private economy. Nevertheless, the imprint of private enterprise is deeply and decisively upon the war-production achievement. The success of the unprecedentedly huge undertaking has been dependent on the initiative, resourcefulness, and ability of private business. Even the government's part in the process has been in large part planned and supervised by men trained in private industry who brought the administrative skills and energies of free capitalism to their task.

Any attempt to interpret war production as a triumph for state operation must miscarry, since it is easy to show that private capitalism carried out the assignment *despite* the handicaps of many government policies curtailing private freedom of action, and *despite* myriad bureaucratic controls. Credit for the most astounding production job in all human history must go primarily to American capitalism. . . .

Frontiers of Expansion

The great depression of the 1930's induced in the American people moods of self-doubt bordering on despair. It looked like the end of the world—the end of the rich, busy, confident, productive American world. Not progress but sheer animal survival emerged as a national ideal. Not opportunity, which is the dynamic element in human society, but security, which is its static element, ruled men's dreams. . . .

It took a catastrophic war to awaken America from its defeatist lethargy. The needs suddenly became so colossal that available goods and plant seemed pathetically small and limited. Far from possessing "more of almost everything than we can use," we discovered that we had less of almost everything than we needed—too little plant capacity, too little oil, too little metals, virtually no rubber, inadequate man power, too little food. We had to take heroic measures to *restrict purchases* and repress appetites for goods, where we had thought our population sated and indifferent.

It took a great war to demonstrate to America that its creative forces, far from being exhausted, had scarcely been touched. The very officials who had repeatedly "proved" that the limits of the nation's productivity had been reached now set gigantic tasks and stood dumb-founded by the speed, the sureness, the efficiency with which these were carried out. It became manifest that immense untapped strength resided in our national muscles, our genius for mass output, our talents for "rationalization" of industrial processes, our resourcefulness in over-coming barriers.

America has only begun to understand its own productive capaci-ties, and one of the most difficult problems of our future is to adjust our thinking to that capacity. Even in our most optimistic periods, it is now clear, we had underestimated our own abilities. In the last twenty years we have raised output per man-hour by about 40 per cent. More signifi-cantly, we have learned that this stepped-up production can be further enlarged as the workers themselves become aware that they have much to gain in the general avalanche of abundance. Under the impact of war demands we have found additional millions of capable working hands. We have found new materials and new uses for old materials, new fecundity in industrial branches thought sterile. We are only at the foot-hills of production, with mountains still to climb.

Our country has been roused out of its nightmare of despair. But remnants of the evil dream—amorphous fears and gnawing doubts—still cling to our minds. The theory of a "mature economy" continues to be preached, almost out of inertia, by influential leaders. They explain that the war proves nothing and that peace will find us again trapped in an overdeveloped and played-out economy.

They believe that opportunity for the private citizen to invest in new enterprises or in expanding old ones, thus creating new jobs, is over. Therefore, they warn us that when the war is ended we should not waste time patching up the existing "mature" system. Instead, they urge, we should set up a new system—one in which business might still be privately owned but wholly dependent on government for its capital, and the superstate will obtain funds through taxation and enlargement of public debt and will plan for industry and manage the carrying out of these plans.

I do not for a moment accept their view. I regard it as a hangover of depression defeatism. Their words and warnings are but echoes of the nightmare. What the American people have done under the artificial impetus of a war challenge they can do again and do better under the living impetus of their determination for a more abundant existence for the whole nation.

The upsurge of energy, inventiveness, productivity evoked by an external enemy can and must be maintained for war against internal enemies such as poverty, low living standards, chronic unemployment. These are challenges as real as the Axis and can be met in the same spirit. . . .

When the War Is Over . . .

We must face the fact that only prison and prison societies are able to provide full employment in the literal sense of the words. Slaves have never been in danger of remaining unemployed. They might be under-fed and underclothed but never underworked. When there is not enough productive labor to keep them busy, they can always be set to building pyramids for the greater glory of their masters.

And the subjects of a modern totalitarian state, by the same token, are rarely in danger of unemployment. Their master, the superstate, can *invent* work to keep them busy. Since their labor power can be exploited ruthlessly, on a bread-and-water diet if necessary, in labor camps if necessary, they are usually sure of keeping busy. Countries in time of war, too, are able to offer full employment, but again by approximating the totalitarian state and accepting for the duration types of "discipline" and dictatorship that would be rejected in normal times.

Any people willing to pay the price—in freedoms, self-respect, and standards of living—can buy literal full employment. The American people can have it for the asking. But I do not believe they are prepared to pay that price. I am convinced that they prefer to take their chances, along with management and agriculture, in a free economy. They do so fully aware that a free economy is a fluctuating economy, with peaks and slumps in employment.

I believe Americans will insist increasingly on making the process as painless as possible, through insurance and other types of social security. They will insist increasingly that management and labor unions, separately and together, strive to forestall sudden slumps by planning ahead, by curbing the kind of dog-eat-dog competition and fevered finance which breed depressions. But they will recognize at the same time that capitalism is not merely a profit system but a profit-*and-loss* system, in which the enterpriser and the laborer alike take risks.

The truth is that we cannot achieve permanent 100 per cent employment without destroying the flexibility of our competitive setup.

As long as capitalism retains its resiliency, its give-and-take, its urge to abandon old methods and products for new ones, we shall have ups and downs in employment. . . .

Freedom from want is basic in the American dream. No other country in history has come so far toward achieving this goal. But in the final analysis that freedom depends on the healthy functioning and continuous growth of our productive processes. To kill off technological progress, to stymie invention and new efficiencies by making them economically hazardous, is really to increase rather than erase want.

Industry and commerce, too, suffer growing pains. But surely no one wants to have them artificially stunted and retarded. Maladjustments in terms of crises in employment, business failures, elimination of the unfit in management and in labor, reconditioning of capital and labor alike to meet new, bigger, more lucrative, and more socially useful tasks —these are inherent in the people's capitalism. . . .

THE LABOR MOVEMENT

American workers made impressive gains during World War II. Full employment and the support of the National War Labor Board caused trade union membership to climb from 10.5 to 14.75 million. By 1944, as a result of wage increases and overtime pay, real weekly wages before taxes in manufacturing were 50 per cent higher than in 1939. The employment of women and teenagers also boosted family living standards. But government efforts to stabilize wages created certain pressures. Although labor had offered a no-strike pledge shortly after Pearl Harbor, the spring of 1943 witnessed a nationwide coal strike and a threatened railroad walkout. This unrest in turn kindled public indignation and led Congress to enact, over Roosevelt's veto, legislation designed to curb wartime strikes and restrict political activity by unions. Although attention tended to center on labor conflict, absenteeism and a high rate of job turnover affected production more seriously than did work stoppages.

14 ★ Louis Stark, "What's the Matter with Labor?"

The coal strike of 1943 and congressional consideration of punitive legislation led Louis Stark, a prominent reporter of labor news, to analyze the relationship between workers' grievances and Administration proposals to restrain inflation. [Survey Graphic, XXXII (July 1943), 277-81. Reprinted by permission of Mrs. Helen Hall Kellogg.]

Several weeks after Pearl Harbor a government-labor-management conference was convened by President Roosevelt. Spokesmen for the American Federation of Labor and the Congress of Industrial Organizations, meeting with a committee of industrialists, agreed that there should be no strikes and no lockouts during the war. They recommended the creation of a National War Labor Board to adjust disputes. The question of the closed shop split the conferees. The labor representatives wished to have the new board consider all disputes, including demands for the closed shop, while the management group was opposed. Before an agreement could be reached on this question, President Roosevelt announced his acceptance of the conference's no-strike-no-lockout policy and its agreement to have a labor board established. His own ruling was that all disputes should go before the board.

On January 12, 1942 the National War Labor Board was created by executive order as a tripartite body of twelve members, equally divided among labor, industry and public representatives, with William H. Davis of New York as chairman. The new board began its work under severe handicaps. The government-labor-industry meeting had not had time to consider problems such as wartime wages, the cost of living, the creation of machinery for limiting "raiding" by competitive unions in war plants and industries, the new factor of women in industry, the training of a new industrial army, the dilution of unskilled and skilled labor. Policies respecting these factors had, therefore, to be improvised by the board itself on a catch-as-catch-can basis as it went along.

At the outset, the board's wage policy was a generous one, with the industry members frequently dissenting. Strikes were kept down fairly well for some months because of two rulings: first, wage adjustments were made retroactive, to the date of the expiration of an agreement or a date otherwise deemed fair; and second, a form of "maintenance of membership" was granted which fell short of the closed shop but which the unions were willing to accept as a working arrangement for the duration.

Each case was considered by the board as a separate affair and its policy was to refrain from general rulings. But the number of cases increased as the months passed and the backlog mounted so rapidly in the spring of 1942 that local unions went on strike despite labor's national no-strike pledge.

The labor board's policy was not to consider disputes while the employes were on strike. Promises to consider the cases promptly resulted in the end of these walkouts. However, the "good" unions which had waited patiently for rulings also became uneasy as the days passed and in many cases were tempted to threaten strikes or to walk out in unofficial stoppages in order to compel quick attention of the board. At the bottom of this unrest lay the rise in living costs and labor's desire to keep in step with it.

A calming effect on labor was applied by President Roosevelt in his announcement of April 27, 1942, calling for a seven-point "indivisible" anti-inflation program designed to keep prices down, to stimulate adequate tax legislation and to stabilize wages. This projected program, however, did not solve the specific difficulties in which the NWLB found itself, due to the rapid increase in the number of disputes. Finally, George W. Taylor, professor of labor relations at the Wharton School and vice-chairman of the board, worked out a formula, which, it was presumed, could be invoked in a general way to administer wage adjustments on a fair basis and on a more or less wholesale pattern.

The formula, applied first on July 6, 1942 in the case of four steel companies and known as the "Little Steel" formula, was simple. Living costs, according to the U.S. Bureau of Labor Statistics, had risen 15 per cent between January 1, 1941 and May 1942. The formula provided that all who had not been accorded a 15 per cent increase in straight time hourly rates between those dates, were regarded as entitled to such an adjustment. The board considered the formula generous, based as it was on hourly earnings, for the number of work hours had increased in the meantime and overtime rates had also added considerable [sic] to the weekly "take home." Labor members of the board opposed the "Little Steel" formula but were somewhat mollified by the liberal interpretations of the formula by the public members. During this phase of the formula's application, wage adjustments beyond 15 per cent were made on the basis of "gross inequities," "inequalities," maladjustments of living costs and those necessary to aid in the effective prosecution of the war.

Then came the Act of October 2, 1942 which placed a ceiling on wages and farm prices. The NWLB was empowered to carry out the provisions of the new wage stabilization act in so far as it affected hourly wage earners and all but certain salaried employes earning less than $5,000 a year.

The day after the anti-inflation act was adopted by Congress, the President named James F. Byrnes as Director of Economic Stabilization, and from this moment on labor's back began to rise, because he formulated regulations calling for strict application of the "Little Steel" formula. Any proposed wage increases from May 1942 to September 1942 were to be ignored since wages as of September 15, 1942 were to be considered fair.

Now began for the NWLB a heavy double duty, that of adjusting wartime labor disputes and also of carrying out a national wage stabilization policy simultaneously. The board was by this time already flooded with additional labor disputes. Its new regional offices were soon choked with applications for wage adjustments aside from those requested in the dispute cases. Every employer who wished to make a voluntary wage adjustment had to receive permission from the wage stabilization officers of the labor board. The members of the board were willing to take on these duties. There was some opinion in the Administration that separate national wage stabilization machinery should be created to relieve the board of this additional burden, but this was not done.

In the meantime other things were happening on the price and job front to irritate the labor organizations. Commodity costs of essential foodstuffs were rising despite the efforts of the Office of Price Administration, and rationing controls were proving not to be as effective as desired. At the same time, the War Manpower Commission, by new regulations restricting the migration of labor, began moving in the direction of what labor felt was job "freezing."

By the spring of 1943 the Administration was convinced that increased purchasing power bearing on the dwindling supply of goods threatened to wreck its anti-inflation program. The result was President Roosevelt's "hold the line" order of April 8, 1943. This order was designed as a "tough" wage policy and it was, for it changed the "rules" by eliminating all reasons for wage adjustments except those made in accord with the "Little Steel" formula and to cover maladjustments in living standards. No longer was the board able to adjust wages because of "inequalities" or "gross inequities" or for purposes related to the effective prosecution of the war. Overnight some 17,000 wage cases, many of which had been waiting action by the board for months, were wiped out.

Having waited months for wage adjustments which had been in the NWLB hopper, employes were disgruntled. For example, a West Coast lumber commission set up by the NWLB had granted a wage increase to one group of lumber workers and the applications of other groups were "in the works." The latter, however, had to be denied under the new policy and the employes affected felt that they were just as worthy as their fellows who had had the advantage of an earlier decision.

Unauthorized strikes grew in number as labor spokesmen insisted that the NWLB no longer was a "judicial" body for it was now using a "mechanical yardstick" to adjust wages. The post-Pearl Harbor labor-industry conference had agreed that each case was to be considered on its merits, and now by substituting a "rigid formula" the government was alleged to have broken the agreement it had made. So ran the argument. John L. Lewis, president of the United Mine Workers, plunged into the fight. His was the most extreme position for he declared frankly he was out to smash the NWLB as he had its predecessor. Under the "Little Steel" formula he knew his miners were not entitled to any wage increase and they had scant hope for more money under the "hold the line" order. This was but one of the NWLB's recurrent crises.

The "hold the line" order, however, was modified by interpretation several weeks after it had been issued, but only after both the AFL and the CIO had given strong indications that they would withdraw their representatives from the NWLB if the order were permitted to stand in its original form. Sufficient authority was returned by Mr. Byrnes to the NWLB to reassure the board that it was a "judicial" rather than an administrative body. It was permitted to adjust wages if "gross inequities" were involved or if changes were called for to aid in "the effective prosecution of the war" or to correct maladjustments in living standards. These concessions, however, were hedged about with provisions that nullified such adjustments if price increases were required. Mr. Byrnes also provided that an elaborate study of wage classifications be made and used as a yardstick to adjust below-minimum wages.

Despite these concessions, labor is still pressing for further adjustments. The AFL would discard the "Little Steel" formula in any event, feeling that even under the modification of the "hold the line" order, labor is unable to obtain fair consideration of its wage demands. The CIO would have the President withdraw from the Office of Economic Stabilization, now commanded by Judge Fred M. Vinson, authority to review NWLB adjustments made to eliminate "gross inequities" or to "aid in the effective prosecution of the war" and to make the labor board the final authority in all such adjustments of wage rates. . . .

Labor's dissatisfaction with the administration's wage and price policies, its resentment over some of the so-called "job freezing" regulations issued by the War Manpower Commission, and lack of union discipline have led to an increase in the number of unauthorized strikes. These factors, together with two nation-wide coal strikes within a month, resulted in the drastic Connally-Smith bill, which provides for supervision of strike votes, fines and imprisonment for those instigating strikes in war plants operated or seized by the government, registration of unions, the filing of data on their finances and the prohibition of union contributions to political parties.

15 ★ Debate on the No-Strike Pledge

The no-strike pledge given by leaders of the AFL and CIO caused some misgivings among the rank and file. In 1942, the Michigan CIO Council endorsed the pledge, but a year later it approved a motion recommending that "unless the assurances that were made to labor at the time we gave up our right to strike" were honored, the pledge should be nullified. The debate pointed up the conflicting attitudes of workers in wartime. [Sixth Annual Convention of the Michigan CIO Council, *Proceedings* (June 30, 1943), 136-45. Reprinted by permission of State AFL-CIO Council.]

Delegate Ruth Biggin (Local 208, UAWA): Mr. Chairman, I think this resolution is an insult to Phil Murray, to President Roosevelt and to all the win-the-war forces and labor organization itself and to all labor people who are interested in winning the war. . . .

I think this resolution should be defeated. I came here in the interest of extending the CIO program and policy for winning the war. Also, the policy did not say that provided the Smith-Connally Bill was defeated we would lift the no-strike ban. It recognized that there might be a probability that the Smith-Connally Bill might be defeated. It did not say that if that happens, the no-strike ban would be lifted.

We had better wake up and find out if we are interested in winning the war. Two wrongs don't make a right. I think we should redouble our efforts to win the war and give our support to Murray, Roosevelt and the win-the-war forces. (Applause and cheers and boos)

Delegate Reynolds (Dodge Local No. 3): Mr. Chairman, I rise to support the resolution. I believe that we of labor should stay on the side of labor. The reactionary forces are trying to have us vote down this resolution which takes away the right of labor to get its rightful gains and the only way to get those gains, and there isn't any use of kidding ourselves, is by striking. I don't believe we should strike these plants unless we absolutely have to. You can take the Chrysler workers. Chrysler workers are underpaid. We have our contract. We have been trying to get a contract for some six or seven months out of the War Labor Board and what do we get. We get just a plain run around! When we had a three-day stoppage, the War Labor Board promised us that they would get the Chrysler contract out of the red tape that it is meshed down in Washington inside of two weeks. Here it is going into another five or six weeks and we still have not a contract. The Chrysler workers are underpaid. They want an impartial umpire and various other things. What have we got in the past year? When we have the no-strike pledge and went along with our pledge, our people were fired. Our people are still on the street. When we had that three day stoppage we wanted them to upgrade people, people with seniority, people that have a right to be upgraded. The company goes out on the street hiring, hiring for the good jobs and leaving the people with seniority on those lower priced jobs. We asked the company to go along with us but when they refused to give anything, when we shut down for three days, they were damned glad to do it. During the course of the past year they acquired people, but after this three day stoppage they said they were going to discharge some other brothers. We told them if you discharge anybody else, we will close all your plants down. As a result of that there has not been anybody fired.

The corporation that I work for knows only one language and that is the language of strike, and there isn't any one in this convention that can say they can deal with the Chrysler Corporation on any other terms. The only language they understand is the language of strike, and I say, let's give it to them.

(Boos and applause)

PRESIDENT SCHOLLE: In order to provide opportunity for people to speak for and against the resolution, I would like to suggest that the next speaker be one who is opposed to the resolution.

DELEGATE PAUL WEBER (American Newspaper Guild): Brother President, I am speaking against the resolution.

I find myself in strange and unaccustomed company. However, Brothers, it is necessary to take positions on the acts as you see them. It seems to me that no better argument against this resolution can be made than the address of Brother Reynolds who stated that he had gone on strike in the Chrysler plant, that is men were still on the street, and the total net result of that has been that the case had been taken to the War Labor Board. . . .

I would like also to make this point,—that when you strike in a war industry, you do not damage the management. Unfortunately, that is true. I think Chrysler exemplified that fact. The company has a contract with the government for X number of guns and they don't care whether you make those guns in six weeks or eight weeks. The only one hurt is the future of the labor movement and the capacity of the armed forces that defend us all.

And on those grounds I am opposed to the resolution. (Applause and cheers) . . .

DELEGATE JOHN COLE (Local 50, UAWA): Mr. Chairman, this motion, to my mind, brings up the very best in all of us. One thing you have listened to during the entire proceedings here has been jockeying into positions. You have heard a lot of technicalities. I am going to talk to you in your own terms on your motion. A lot of you know what pressure groups are, and I don't care what you say our efforts have been sabotaged along these lines by pressure groups in the Congress and the Senate. We do know that Phil Murray and Green of the AFL have been pressured into making these statements that they want a no-strike pledge. (Boos) True enough. It's a fact. I am going to tell you this one thing . . . but the threat of a strike is a two-edged sword. It hits right back. In Congress they have stabbed our efforts on equality of sacrifice. In the convention in Chicago I went along. But the manufacturers association have also sabotaged this effort by having the salary limitations withdrawn and now salaries have skyrocketted and as you know there is no equality of sacrifice in that.

Our Local 50 is going along with this a thousand per cent due to the fact we don't want dictation. You are going to be dictated to. Let's not be dictated to by Phil Murray and Green. I am going to stick along with the President of the United States. He has shown inclination against this strike pledge but no strike has come to attention in these words. He has not given anyone that he likes this pledge. Let's use this effort and let's use this opportunity at this time to get back at management and get back at Congress and give them the threat that is so necessary. Don't lose your individuality. Don't give it up. A no-strike pledge at this time is going to do one thing, going to let us down, we are going to be jockeyed into position by pressure groups and run along to their way of doing. Don't let this happen in the labor movement here. Let this entire group go as fighting for the individual—

PRESIDENT SCHOLLE: Time.

The next speaker shall be one against the adoption of the resolution.

DELEGATE WASHINGTON (Local 600, UAWA): I represent approximately 90,000 workers, (Boos) the majority of whom are against striking at this time because we recognize that it is important that the people who are fighting in South Africa, North Africa, Guadalcanal, need the things which we make. I also feel that as a member of the International Union of Auto Workers, the majority of whom have already gone on record as against striking at this time, do not feel that such a resolution should be supported. And those locals who were named as presenting the resolution are in the minority in the Auto Workers.

R. J. Thomas, a vice-president of the CIO, spoke yesterday and he pointed out that we should not forget the one important thing at this time is the winning of the war and Philip Murray has pointed out time and time again we are not hurting management, as a previous speaker spoke when we do that. We are hurting ourselves. We are taking things away from our boys who are on the battle lines the products of labor that they need to protect themselves and win this war. And I want to urge all of you who are Americans, who are with the allied nations, who are sincere in wanting to see this war won that you vote down this resolution and continue to give your support to the Administration. (Applause and Cheers) . . .

DELEGATE LUCAS: Brother Chairman and Brothers and Sisters: In the first place this resolution does not revoke the no-strike pledge. It is only a question of certain policy and advising with the National CIO as to how we feel on this particular question. And what group has a better right to advise with the National CIO than the Michigan CIO?

Some time ago labor made a very noble gesture. That was a matter of giving a no-strike pledge. Arguments to the contrary notwithstanding, there were certain commitments that were made to labor at that particular time. Does anyone in this hall question that these commitments have not been lived up to by the administration? I don't think that we can honestly say that the administration has done the things that [it] stated would be done at the time of giving the no-strike pledge.

Now, in the first place, we state that labor made the no-strike pledge. The no-strike pledge was given and then brought to the "Equality of Sacrifice" conference of the United Automobile Workers and [they] told us there that they wanted us to follow up a line laid down and give our unstinted support. At that time I voted in favor of it. And there is an old saying that wise men change their minds but fools never do. Now I have become convinced that the giving of the no-strike pledge was the biggest mistake that labor has ever made. (Applause and boos) You have only to look into your own particular plant and see what your conditions, your collective bargaining set up is. Are the managements bargaining in these plants?

(Voices: No)

I certainly don't think they are. When it comes to question of giving labor its just due, it seems that the administration seems to not be able to find any money to do anything with but when it comes to the question of building plants for corporations who have already more than they need, they can find billions of dollars to do that with. Is that giving labor a square deal? I don't think so. My personal sentiments are on this question that the no-strike pledge should be revoked here and now. (Applause and boos and time called) . . .

DELEGATE BOATIN: We were told that this resolution was only a threat. The same person who made that statement from the committee, wound up two minutes afterwards by telling that we should revoke our no-strike pledge here and now. And I think the bankruptcy of their position is revealed in their own words. Who wants the revocation? By whom will it be welcome? Hitler and Tojo, undoubtedly.

Surely we have grievances. Surely the manufacturers create numerous grievances for us, and why? And who in particular are these manufacturers? In the majority of cases the manufacturers [who] create numerous grievances are the ones who are not interested in winning the war. They create these grievances, they help to create these grievances and refuse to negotiate primarily because they want us to go on strike, so we can have a negotiated peace, so Hitler can continue in war and so we can have Hitlerism in this country. A strike would be against our men who are on the battlefields, against the entire labor movement, against the very war we are fighting. The revocation of the no-strike pledge will not solve the problem. Brother Reynolds indicated that it did not solve their problem. Strikes will not establish democracy in the world. . . .

DELEGATE VICTOR REUTHER (Local 174, UAW): Brother Chairman, it is amazing what strange conclusions can be drawn from a very simple resolution. I think wrong conclusions are being drawn by speakers speaking both for and against. I want to speak on the resolution and for the resolution as it is written, not as it has been interpreted by some.

I would be opposed now in view of the existing CIO policy for the immediate revocation of our no-strike pledge because I respect the democratic procedure in CIO and that is why I believe, as a member of this organization I have the right to join with others in recommending what in my honest opinion is best for our labor movement.

No one has answered the question here of what we should do to get management to bargain collectively or to get government agencies to respect the problems we have under war time conditions, or to give us advice, give labor representation in government agencies.

This move, this recommendation would have far more effect upon the War Labor Board than upon management. I am aware of that. I appreciate the position of Phil Murray. If I were in his shoes I wish I would have the same courage to do what he did. I also appreciate that President Murray needs the honesty and frankness of the guys back in the shop to open the eyes of Washington and let them know that our people think that problem must be solved now and not six years from now. (Applause)

I do not believe that President Murray has designated individuals throughout the group to act as spokesmen. He speaks for himself, and I will make this clear, I think we ought to face issues fairly and squarely and not to cover up our own hidden motives by saying "Roosevelt is in favor of it," "Murray is in favor of it."

I appreciate the things Roosevelt has done but I condemn him for other suggestions—the suggestion of drafting strikers. I don't go along with that and I will speak against it. (Applause)

I think in this instance, the guys back in the shops ought to suggest to government that it take seriously the problems that it faces, the roll back of prices and so on. Others will say that it is against CIO policy to tell the government,—by God! they've got to give us concessions in terms of roll back—

(Time called by the Chairman)

I will conclude—

PRESIDENT SCHOLLE: Time is called.

(There were cries for the Question and demands for the floor.)

PRESIDENT SCHOLLE: Are there fifty or more that wish the previous question? All those in favor of the previous question will please say "Aye"; Opposed "No". The motion to act on the resolution is carried.

All those in favor of the adoption of the resolution will please rise.

All those opposed will stand.

The Chair is in doubt.

(Cries for Roll Call Vote)

All those who favor adoption will rise.

All those opposed to the resolution please stand.

The resolution is carried.

AGRICULTURAL CHANGE

War transformed agriculture no less than industry and labor. First, it led to a sharp decline in farm population; between 1940 and 1945, 5 million farm dwellers—17 per cent of the total—moved from the land. Submarginal farmers and tenants were particularly attracted by opportunities in industry and the armed forces. Second, the productivity of each farmer increased by more than 25 per cent. This resulted from increased mechanization, consolidation of small farms into large ones, greater crop diversification, favorable weather conditions, high prices, and a dramatic rise in the use of fertilizer. Finally, war touched the farmer with prosperity. As their cash income jumped from $2.3 billion in 1940 to nearly $9.5 billion in 1945, farmers paid off mortgages and put aside savings. Of course, war exacted a toll in the form of displaced families, deteriorating rural schools, and depleted forest resources; on balance, though, it improved the farmer's position.

16 ★ A New York Farmer and the War

The war brought with it certain changes, and accelerated others, on the dairy and general farm run by Daniel Carey in Groton, New York. Carey, who was closely associated with the farmer's cooperative movement, later served as Assistant to the Secretary of Agriculture (1948-1952) and Commissioner of the New York State Agricultural Department (1955-1959). In the following interview, conducted by Dr. Gould P. Colman of the Cornell Program in Oral History in 1967, Carey discusses some of the ways in which the war affected his farming operation. (Editorial deletions in the oral transcript are indicated by ellipses.) [Daniel Carey Memoir, Cornell Program in Oral History, pp. 290-91, 294-95, 300-01. Reprinted by permission of Mr. Carey.]

CAREY: Our operation was really somewhat static previous to the war period. We had gone through the twenties and the depression of the thirties and having purchased two farms in the early twenties and hitting the financial depression of that period, about the only reason why they left me on the farm, I guess, during the depression period was because nobody else would run it. You wouldn't get money enough to pay the interest on the mortgage. But, after that we began to revive again and we moved into . . . the late thirties, when we began to pick up a little; we accumulated considerable equipment and a herd of cows and in the early forties, I believe '41, '42, and '43, particularly 1943, we had very good years—prices were rising and we were able to catch up, at least, on our indebtedness and get in financial condition where we could move. So that as far as our own operation was concerned, we had just about gotten, when the prices began to increase, to the point where we could take advantage of those increases in prices. We had the two farms of about two hundred and seventy acres, two hundred and seventy-five acres; in 1945 we purchased a neighboring farm of one hundred acres and began to expand a little at that time. We raised more heifers, enlarged our dairy. Then, fertilizer, we were able to purchase more fertilizer, raise better crops, we began to take out more hedgerows and do strip-cropping, begin to get into conservation work. We knew, all the time, that we needed to use more lime and more fertilizer, but previous to the thirties—previous to the Roosevelt administration, when they began the overall program of converting from crops, row crops, and soil depleting crops to soil conserving crops, grasses and so forth— . . . [we] just didn't have the dollars to buy it. And during that period of time we began to get the dollars where we could buy more and more on our own. . . . As I recall, we were able to obtain, during that period, about all the fertilizer and lime and so forth that we could buy. . . .

COLMAN: How about labor during the war?

CAREY: Well, we were quite fortunate, of course, our youngsters were growing up at that time, we had . . . three boys and we had three girls and they were all pretty good helpers around the farm. At that time we raised about, oh, ten or a dozen acres of potatoes and about the same amount of cabbage. And then, just about the war time, there was quite a demand for canning factory peas . . . and we would raise as much as fifteen acres of peas. . . . We would have all these potatoes to cultivate and handle, and our corn to cultivate, and cabbage to plant, and the peas would come on, we'd have a terrific amount of work. So we had arranged at that time with the college . . . and for a number of years we had boys from the college who worked out here during the summer months. . . .

COLMAN: How about spare parts? Did you have any trouble on that?

CAREY: I don't believe we did. We had a good company that we dealt with at that time, . . . and we had very little trouble with parts. We didn't have to replace too much equipment because in the few years previous to that I had purchased quite a lot of machinery. I'd purchased it on time, all of it, . . . the only way I could have bought it at that time, but we were pretty well equipped with equipment at that time. Enough so that we got through the war period, in pretty good shape.

COLMAN: You spoke a moment ago about off-farm work. . . . Was this something that many of your neighbors did, worked off the farm during the war?

CAREY: No. No. There were a number of small farms around, oh, seven or eight cows, or ten cows, and they worked for L. C. Smith and Corona typewriter. . . . They took all the help that they could get, so a lot of these small fellows worked with them, but not the larger farmers. . . . But there had been quite a transition, there was quite a transition even at that time on the, oh, I guess, maybe three miles of road that runs from the end of Main, South Main Street in Groton around to the McLean Road Harbor Road. There were fifteen farms producing milk when I started in farming in 1919. And I would expect that by this time there weren't over half a dozen of those farms producing milk.

COLMAN: You mean at the beginning of the war or at the end of the war?

CAREY: The beginning of the war. And now there're really only three farms producing milk. . . .

COLMAN: The consolidation then . . . was occurring well before the war, and that just continued . . .

CAREY: Yes. Just continued.

17 ★ The National Grange Program

During the war, the National Grange increased its membership and, under the leadership of Albert Goss, took an active part in national politics. Speaking for the larger, more prosperous farmer, the Grange remained suspicious of welfare legislation but committed to government support for agriculture. The following address, delivered by Goss on November 11, 1942, expressed the grievances and aspirations of many farmers. [National Grange of the Patrons of Husbandry, Journal of Proceedings, 76th Annual Session (1942), 1-21. Reprinted by permission.]

The farmer's particular responsibility is to produce the food and fiber necessary to win the war. This he has done, and this he will continue to do to the extent of his ability. For years, due to lack of a sound marketing system, farmers suffered from the effects of surplus production. Yet when war came and they were asked to increase production, they did not hesitate, they did not quibble over prices, hours of labor, overtime or guarantees on investment. They went to work and have produced the two largest crops in history. They met and exceeded almost every goal set for them. Unfortunately, however, this cannot be kept up, and unless something is done, food production will fall off sharply. We have had surplus crops so long that we seem to have taken it for granted that they would continue and no adequate safeguards have been provided to give farmers the protection necessary to secure needed production. With the increased consumption, serious food shortages loom in many lines. Farm labor, the Selective Service, priorities and price control all contribute to this problem and will be discussed separately. Altogether it would appear that if we had deliberately gone about it to destroy farm production, we could not have done much worse than we have done in developing our policies on man power and price control. . . .

Price Control

Inflation springs from economic dislocations which interfere in the normal operation of the law of supply and demand. It can best be cured by restoring normal economic processes rather than resorting to mandates of law which require policing. Inflation comes from pressure of excess purchasing power upon an insufficient supply of consumer goods, and results in bidding up prices, which in turn increases costs and starts an upward spiral.

Our efforts at inflation control have been pitifully superficial. They have ignored causes and treated symptoms. To begin with, we have adopted labor policies which have increased costs and curtailed production. We have entered into many billions of dollars in cost-plus contracts which have put a premium on waste and extravagance and enabled the contractors to drain labor from all industries not so favored. The free play of economic law would rectify this by increased wages in the industries whose men have been taken and by increased selling prices to meet the increased cost. However, we have prevented such economic adjustment by providing that when costs increase, industrial wages shall increase proportionally. This is referred to as the Little Steel principle, and is the very essence of inflation. We have attempted control by putting ceilings on prices. Again this is treating symptoms rather than the cause. In fact, it but aggravates the cause. It has been tried time and again; yet in all world history has never succeeded over an extended period. It has resulted in curtailing production, black markets, and finally chaos.

War inevitably causes costly economic dislocations. Draining the ablest of our young men into the armed service increases costs at home. Transportation jams, lack of machinery or repairs, and a thousand other dislocations unavoidably cause cost increases. These increases cannot be prevented by controlling prices. They are a natural accompaniment of war and must be met. Offsetting them is more work, more business and more income. In most instances increased income will more than offset increased costs, but whether or not this is the case, the increased costs must be met, and of course will lower our purchasing power, or standard of living to the extent they are met. We should have political courage enough to meet this issue squarely and permit prices to rise sufficiently to meet such increased costs. Price control should operate to prevent any pyramiding of such increases or profiteering on them. If profiteering is thus controlled, dislocation costs would not be heavy. Such increase will not lead to inflation unless we try to increase income to meet these unavoidable dislocation costs.

The surest cure for inflation is an abundance of production. This can be achieved only by allowing producers to receive production costs. Even then, it cannot always be achieved, due to shortage of raw materials or labor. When scarcity in supply occurs, price ceilings do not increase the supply. They merely maintain the demand. In case of unavoidable shortage, rationing is the most practical course. Rationing assures that rich and poor alike will get all the supplies available on the basis of equality. However, rationing should not be practiced in lieu of a program which would secure ample production if production costs were allowed. . . .

Subsidies may be justified as an aid or incentive to secure abnormal production in special cases where costs are too high to permit production normally. This is a very different principle from employing them to hold down the general price level to consumers. When so employed, the effect is to pass on to the government part of our normal living costs. This form of socialism is wholly unjustifiable.

Priorities

The supply of fertilizer and farm machinery and equipment is short. We cannot expect to get all we want or need, for the needs of our armed forces and those engaged in other essential industries exceed the supply. This is a contributing factor to a reduced food supply. All we can ask is that the need for food, and the supplies and equipment necessary to produce it, be properly evaluated with other essential needs so that a balance be maintained which will be most effective in winning the war. To date this has not been adequately done.

The Selective Service

At the outset of the Selective Service, agriculture was not considered an essential industry, so all eligible farm boys were classed in 1-A, without regard for the nature of their work. Last December, however, as the need for dairy products and certain fats became apparent, regulations were promulgated defining certain crops as essential war crops and certain types of employment as necessary. From time to time those regulations have been modified in an effort to hold the men on the farm, but the original classification has not been changed in many instances, and the calls have been made on the basis of the number of 1-A men on the list. The drain to industry and to enlistment has been mentioned. Too frequently this was not recognized in the calls, so a heavily disproportionate share fell on the farms, and local boards, anxious to meet their quotas, have been too often hard-boiled in taking men essential to maintain production. With between 400,000 and 500,000 idle people in New York City alone, many on relief, and many eligible for the service, it has seemed unjust, and extremely short-sighted, to levy so heavily on the farms before the city surplus was exhausted. To make matters worse, most farm boys wanted to go and it was hard to convince them or their sweethearts that it was more necessary to milk cows and feed hogs at this particular time than to carry a gun.

There is a great economic waste in taking skilled workers from the farm and then attempting to replace them with untrained men. Immediate steps should be taken to grant automatic deferment to all necessary skilled farm workers who cannot be replaced by men of satisfactory training and skill. Agriculture should not ask blanket deferment, but the importance of preserving the food supply of the Nation demands that the necessary labor supply of this industry be protected against further inroads. . . .

In industrial labor the practice of measuring all men with a common rule has evils which are serious enough, but in the case of farm labor the situation is much more aggravated. There is no way of measuring the amount of work the farm employee does, and in many instances the time he works. He usually must turn his hand to the task to be done at any time or in any way. His relations with his employer are frequently more like a partner than like an employee. He is often taken into the home and treated like one of the family. All these things are not susceptible to measurement by any known rule. That is why farm labor was exempted from the provisions of the Wagner Labor Relations Act, the Fair Labor Standards Act, and the Social Security Act. It will be a sorry day for farm labor and for agriculture when it is subjected to uniform rules and regulations.

The Grange feels that the only solution of the farm man power problem is a price for farm crops which will enable farmers to pay what labor is worth. Such prices should enable farmers to pay relatively more for labor than in the past, for farm wages have never been able to compete with factory wages in securing the best men.

Farm Labor

For many years farm labor, when compared with industrial labor, has been underpaid. When measured by the price of farm products or by farm income it has been rather generously paid in most areas, although it varies greatly in different sections of the country. This is not saying that farm wages have been too high, for that is not true. It is but another way of saying that farm income has been too low. Farm wages have generally gone up and down with farm income. . . .

It is only natural that the better income, combined with the shorter hours of labor and time and a half for overtime, should drain the men from the farms into industry. . . .

As a result of this drain, farm production has suffered severely in some areas, and there is a great deal of evidence that plantings for next year will be sharply curtailed. Dairy cows have gone to the slaughter-block in alarming numbers, while farm sellouts have been breaking all records. Although the Grange has been warning the Administration and Congress of this for many months, until recently our warnings have been ignored and we have been blindly plunging into a situation which can result in no other way than a food shortage. When we tried to have this situation partially recognized and partially corrected in the recent price control bill, the farmers were subjected to the most vicious campaign of propaganda, misrepresentation and name-calling seen in years, because we asked that increased farm labor costs be recognized in setting ceilings on farm prices.

3 Politics in Wartime

THE SURVIVAL OF PARTISAN APPEAL

Both major political parties sought to turn the war to their advantage: Democrats called for a truce in the interest of national unity and Republicans affirmed the need for constructive criticism. Not only did the war fail to bring about an end to partisan conflict; it also caused many new issues to emerge and altered existing political alignments. Debate came to center on regulation of the economy, control of inflation, administration of war programs, and the nature of postwar international commitments. Republican victories in the election of 1942 greatly enhanced the influence of the conservative coalition in Congress. Although talk of a possible coalition government arose at various times and Roosevelt brought some Republicans into the Administration, so long as elections were held and competing interests sought to influence government policy the continuation of partisan controversy was unavoidable.

18 ★ *Robert H. Taft,* The Republican Party and the War

To Republicans like Robert Taft of Ohio, who believed that "the New Dealers are determined to make the country over under the cover of war if they can," the need for continued surveillance of the Administration seemed apparent. In a speech made on December 26, 1941, Taft defended the legitimacy of wartime opposition and attempted to define the bounds governing acceptable criticism. [Congressional Record, 77th Cong., 1st Sess., LXXXVII, Part 14, A57099-11.]

Ladies and gentlemen, the United States is at war. For months the people have differed on the question of our foreign policy—whether or not we should risk war to aid Britain; whether or not we should deliberately enter the war. That question has been settled. It may be an interesting theoretical discussion today as to who was right and who was wrong, but we can and we should adjourn that discussion and leave it to history to decide. The position of interventionists and noninterventionists alike was always consistent with 100 per cent support of any war which did occur. Past differences are forgotten by 95 per cent of the people. They should be forgotten by all. . . .

When war came, the country was already largely on a war basis, but many other measures must be taken. I, like all other Members of Congress, have been faced at once by a whole series of new measures raising the question of our proper attitude toward steps proposed by the national administration. How far should Congress accept blindly the measures presented and the powers and finances requested by the Executive and the Army and the Navy? How far should we surrender our own views to hasten any war program approved by the President? Members of the minority party are faced particularly by the problem whether they should criticize the administration of the war—either the legislative measures proposed or the actual conduct of the war itself. These are not easy problems to decide.

As a matter of general principle, I believe there can be no doubt that criticism in time of war is essential to the maintenance of any kind of democratic government. Perhaps nothing today distinguishes democratic government in England so greatly from the totalitarianism of Germany as the freedom of criticism which has existed continuously in the House of Commons and elsewhere in England. Of course, that criticism should not give any information to the enemy. But too many people desire to suppress criticism simply because they think that it will give some comfort to the enemy to know that there is such criticism. If that comfort makes the enemy feel better for a few moments, they are welcome to it as far as I am concerned, because the maintenance of the right of criticism in the long run will do the country maintaining it a great deal more good than it will do the enemy, and will prevent mistakes which might otherwise occur. President Wilson once said that criticism in time of war was even more necessary than in time of peace. Justice Holmes said in one of his brilliant opinions in the Supreme Court: "We do not lose our right to condemn either measures or men because the country is at war." . . .

There will be newspapers and others in my State who will attack me unless I accept the leadership and recommendations of the President on every issue. I cannot find any authority for such a course. The duties imposed by the Constitution on Senators and Congressmen certainly require that we exercise our own judgment on questions relating to the conduct of the war. They require that we do not grant to the President every power that is requested unless that power has some relation to the conduct of the war. They require that we exercise our own judgment on questions of appropriations to determine whether the projects recommended have a real necessity for the success of the war. Certainly Congress must determine questions of fiscal policy.

Nevertheless every problem must be approached in a different spirit from that existing in time of peace, and Congress cannot assume to run the war. Hardly a measure comes before us relating to the Army or the draft which does not raise a question as to the size of the army which we must prepare. . . . I recognize that we must prepare for every effort which may under any circumstances be necessary to bring the war to a conclusion. If military men tell me, therefore, that an army of seven or eight million might be necessary, I shall vote for such an army and as much equipment as the administration deems necessary for such an army. On the other hand, I believe it is my duty to ask the Army how fast they can and will build up that army and how many men are necessary now. I believe Congress must determine the question of policy as to which ages and classes of men should be drafted. That is not a military question, but one of national policy. We do not wish to get an army any faster than we can absorb and train and equip it. . . .

There can't be any business as usual, but we have established in America a great many real values, a standard of living which contributes to the health, welfare, education, and future success of every man and woman, and these should not be lightly abandoned except when it is really necessary for the purposes of the war and the planned conduct of the war. There is no reason to upset every normal relationship until it is necessary. There is no use in throwing thousands of men out of work in small industries if by spreading the manufacture of equipment over a slightly longer period we do not in fact delay the final effort. I see no use in sending boys of 19 or 20 to war unless it is necessary to draft boys of that age in order to get enough men. . . .

Congress does have the job of reasonable criticism. I think it has the job of criticizing the conduct of the war when it is properly subject to criticism. The surprise at Hawaii should, in my opinion, be investigated by committees of Congress, and not left entirely to the executive department. We might well investigate whether Secretary Hull told Secretary Knox the contents of the note which he submitted to the Japanese Government 10 days before, requiring them to withdraw from China, and which was not published until after the attack on Hawaii. Did Secretary Knox communicate to the admiral that we had sent an ultimatum to Japan which in all probability they would not accept? Perhaps the fault at Hawaii was not entirely on the admirals and generals.

Then I believe we should face the economic facts even before they are partially brought home to us by the tax bills of March 15. The expenditures required for an all-out war, 10,000,000 men, and unlimited supplies for twice that number in our Army and other armies, are utterly incredible. They mean a complete dislocation of industry. They mean the destruction of many businesses built up over a long period, and the suspension of many others, although there will be full use for those who are thrown out of work. For years we are going to be regimented, our prices fixed, our lives directed, our incomes reduced. . . .

A strong fiscal policy can reduce somewhat the dangers that we face. Nondefense expenditures can certainly be cut. I believe that within 6 months we can abolish Work Projects Administration and Civilian Conservation Corps and National Youth Administration. We can avoid the billion dollars' worth of pork-barrel projects now in the public-works bill. A tremendous difference can be made if the defense program itself is administered with avoidance of waste. Congress is hardly in a position to do that, but the executive departments can if they will.

On the other hand, an unsound fiscal policy may bring the country to bankruptcy and complete inflation. That has been the result of many wars in many nations. Secretary Morgenthau has taken a correct stand in favor of reducing the Government deficit, reducing expenses and increasing taxes, but unfortunately he is not predominant in the present administration. The Government economists at the heart of the New Deal are just as strong for the theory of Government spending today as they have been during the past 10 years.

That is the kind of nonsense which inspires the present post-war planning within the administration and affects its present fiscal policy. If that kind of philosophy does dominate the Government's policy, we will be ruined long before the war is over. Mr. Eccles, Mr. Henderson, Mr. Currie, and Mr. Mordecai Ezekiel all believe in the efficacy of Government spending. Fortunately, Congress does not agree with them in theory, although it sometimes does in practice. Congress, therefore, has the task of constantly guarding the soundness of the difficult war policy. I hope that we may well perform it. After the first World War we returned rapidly to the basic system of American freedom and free enterprise. We must certainly maintain our system so that that return can again occur when this war ends.

Perhaps I have painted too black a picture. Of course it depends largely on the motives and intentions of those who are administering the Government. But of one thing I am confident. If no effort is made by Congress to combat the steady slide toward government bankruptcy and government operation of business, the picture at the end of the war will be as black as I have painted it. We must do everything possible to win the war, and make every sacrifice that is necessary, but we have the task of preserving the American system of free enterprise. We must grant powers dangerous to freedom and to the Bill of Rights; we cannot help building up a debt dangerous to the safety of the Nation; and yet we can keep constantly in mind the preservation of the fundamentals of our system. We can constantly oppose excessive grants of power not really necessary for the war. We can struggle to reduce the deficit. We can preserve an underlying condition which will permit the administration in power at the end of the war to restore the American system under which we have grown up and in which we believe.

19 ★ Edward J. Flynn, Party Duty in Wartime

> On February 2, 1942, Ed Flynn of the Bronx, chairman of the Democratic National Committee, suggested that voting for Democrats was one way to demonstrate patriotism. On February 6, the President refused to support Flynn by saying: "When a country is at war we want Congressmen, regardless of party—get that—to back up the Government of the United States. . . ." But the meaning of "backing up the Government" was never made plain, and Roosevelt's disclaimer did not prevent Democrats from echoing Flynn's plea. [Congressional Record, 77th Cong., 2nd Sess., LXXXVIII, Part 8, A352-53.]

Webster's Unabridged Dictionary defines criticism as "the act of criticizing, especially unfavorably; censure; also a critical observation, judgment, or review." I am using the definition as is outlined in Webster's Dictionary so that we might have a full understanding of the substance of what criticism really is. The words "a critical observation, judgment, or review," in my opinion, sum up the ordinarily accepted idea of what the word criticism means. Observation or judgment taken alone means nothing. The way to determine the truth of a criticism or judgment is to find the motive which lies behind it, so tonight I would like my hearers to keep in mind primarily the motives of the men who are criticizing and judging at this particular time. Fair criticism—fair judgment—is always welcome. Unfair criticism—unfair judgment—is in itself abhorrent to the American people.

In order to arrive at the motive of the chairman of the Republican National Committee in his address over this station a few weeks ago it is just and proper that we review the record of the majority of Republican Congressmen prior to that fateful day in December when the whole world was shocked beyond words at the disastrous attack of the Japanese Government. . . .

The lend-lease program was fought bitterly by the Republican Party. Mr. MARTIN, as a Member of Congress, if my memory serves me correctly, fought against this measure. When some time ago, a request by the President of the United States was made to fortify the island of Guam, one of our outlying frontiers, Mr. FISH, of the famous firm of Martin, Barton, and Fish, denounced the administration as warmongers attempting to start a conflict where there was no reason for thinking there would be a war. Mr. MARTIN, by his vote concurred in the views of Mr. FISH. Further, Mr. MARTIN voted against the extension of Selective Service and time has proven that this measure was a keystone of our military mobilization program. If the present administration, under the leadership of President Roosevelt, had followed the lead of the majority of the Republican Members of Congress, the present situation would be so deplorable that there would not be words in the English language to describe it. Such is the record, and political maneuvering is still the motive behind the criticisms which are now being levied and will continue to be levied by Republican spokesmen until the elections of 1942.

I am bespeaking no perfection for the present administration's conduct of defense preparations of this country in a war emergency. I do ask, however, for fair judgment insofar as those preparations are concerned and for public recognition that patriotic—not political—considerations have been the conscientious concern of President Roosevelt. Public memory is sometimes short lived, and so I remind you that the President, before the outbreak of war, appointed as Secretary of War one of the most prominent Republicans in the United States, a former member of the Cabinet of President Hoover, whom no doubt some of you will remember. He appointed to the portfolio of the Navy, Mr. Frank Knox, a candidate for the Vice Presidency on the Republican ticket not so many years ago. . . . The Office of Production Management also is overwhelmingly staffed with men whose political affiliations were not Democratic but Republican. Just a few days ago we were advised of the appointment of former Republican Secretary of War Hurley as a brigadier general and as Minister to New Zealand.

This course is nonpartisan. It is unity in the highest degree. This is a coalition government. It is a real coalition government. The President did not take discredited men who were rejected by the people both in the State and in the Nation for public office. He took capable leaders wherever he found them, asking not their politics; asking only whether or not it was possible for them to do the job and to do the job well. . . .

It is a source of great regret to me that Republicans have started the injection of partisan politics into our present situation. Obviously, the Democratic Party cannot remain quiescent while the other fellows are bending their energies to elect Republican representatives to the House and Senate. Our feeling, or at least my feeling as chairman of the national organization, is that this crisis having occurred during a Democratic administration, the responsibility is ours to direct the carrying on of this war to an ultimate and complete victory.

Our loyalty in this direction is not limited to allegiance to our party. It is our duty to our country. I naturally feel that no misfortune except a major military defeat could befall this country to the extent involved in the election of a Congress hostile to the President. I do not mean by this that the Republican candidates for congressional seats have any lack of patriotism, but I think we will all agree that vast confusion would inevitably result if we had a President of one party and a House of Representatives, for example, of the opposition party while we are carrying on the worst war in our history. This is an important factor, also, in the negotiation of final peace. We have not forgotten the obstacles thrown in the path of President Wilson after the first World War and the ultimate victims were the people.

I anticipate no such result, of course, in the congressional elections next November. Our people are too united for anything of that sort to happen, even though the Grand Old Party leadership may take the contrary view. But let us leave the issues to be settled in the congressional races until those races are near at hand. There will be a campaign period in which all phases of this matter can be discussed and during which the American people can examine the record in the light of pre-war opposition and opposition since the declaration of war. Let us consider this present outburst of political oratory in the light of its effect upon our enemies. What can more encourage and hearten the Nazis and the Japanese than constant attempts to discredit and repudiate the President of the United States at this time when every effort is being made to gear our war machines to maximum production and effectiveness? They have preached to their people that ours is a loose Government, that we are divided by factionalism, and that disunion is disrupting our military preparations and our production of arms and munitions. The only beneficiaries of the Republican policy of political criticism, the only celebrants are in Tokyo, on the Axis front in Russia, in Rome, in Berlin, and in other Axis centers. This political policy of unfair criticism can only shock the morale of our own gallant fighters and of all the forces now massed and massing against Hitler's world conquest.

Let us have enough of this hypocrisy. The President of the United States today stands as the leader of a united people. Completely unfounded charges that he has been or is involved in political maneuvering tend to undermine public confidence in him. These false charges represent political propaganda at its worst. . . .

I repeat, these attacks are unfair. Possibly they are but the forerunner of many other attacks which also will be unfair. I bespeak the American people to withhold their judgment until they appraise the motives behind these unfair attacks. The world is looking to us. All of the free people of the world are holding up their hands in prayerful supplication that the liberties that they have fought and bled for may still be preserved. This is no time for pettiness. This is no time for carping criticism. This is no time for politics. This is a time for unity—unity amongst all of our people so that the strength and the wealth and the moral growth of our Nation may be combined together in a supreme effort to again bring liberty to an almost destroyed world.

20 ★ *Harold W. Dodds, "Political Parties in War Time"*

> *Shortly before the election of 1942, Harold W. Dodds, president of Princeton University, stated the case for continuation of political parties. Conceding the dangers inherent in party struggles during wartime, Dodd asserted that in various ways political conflict promoted national unity.* [*The Yale Review*, XXXI (June 1942), 703-12. Copyright by Yale University Press. Reprinted by permission.]

Total war raises anew in urgent form old questions regarding the political processes of democracy in crisis. In our wars of the past the military handicaps of a government resting on discussion and consent have been cancelled out by similar conditions among our enemies. Today we can count on no such help from the other side. As at no time in our history the nation must be able to act as one man. More searchingly than ever before we must ask ourselves this question: In a survival war can we afford the peace-time privilege of political campaigns and elections, involving as seems inevitable party squabbles and politics in high places? Should political parties suspend for the duration? . . .

It is true that the aim of organized parties is to win elections. No party counts practically that cannot elect some of its candidates part of the time. The strategy of the party in power is to praise its own accomplishments, conceal its mistakes and discredit the claims of the minority. Conversely, the usual objective of the minority is to strangle the majority by harassing it constantly. To this end it obstructs and hamstrings the Administration by techniques well known to politicians. It exaggerates the mistakes of the government and strives to sow distrust of it. By winning away its supporters it strives to render the majority helpless. . . .

Further consideration, however, quickly reveals that political parties, with all their imperfections, are indispensable instruments for maintaining political liberty. It is their struggles for power that activate government. Freedom of speech or opinion would be in vain without them to implement our liberties. There appears to be no alternative to elections except tyranny. It is significant that no general sentiment for suspending elections in the coming autumn has developed; and no leader is strong enough today to bring it about if he would. . . .

Since politics are inevitable in a democracy, is it expecting too much that the President as head of the government and the opposition leaders in Congress shall rise above party in war time? In a sense, it is. Cynics to the contrary, many party members believe in their party's principles, although it must be admitted that there is today in the United States a great deal of confusion in this area. More realistic is the fact that the President must formulate his policies and fight for their adoption. This he cannot do without the help of a party organization. On the other hand, it is only through the criticism of the opposition that the Administration can be held up to the mark in efficiency and responsibility. The enormous war powers entrusted to the Executive these days, on top of a decade of expanding administrative jurisdiction, increase rather than decrease the importance of holding him responsible. . . .

American politics are not all skullduggery and slander. Despite their perversions, parties make for national unity. Under our two-party system, they tend to dull the keen edges of issues on which people divide rather than to sharpen them by introducing new causes of disunity. It is to their interest to do so. To be successful in an election, a political organization must be skilful in mediating divergent points of view within its ranks. This compulsion tends to deplete the impact of sectional or factional interests throughout the nation and to effect a common denominator of opinion. Each side wants to gain the support also of the independent middle-of-the-road voters not affiliated with it. As the two parties bid for votes their programs naturally move to the centre. This influence is one service of the two-party system as against the multi-party habits which prevailed on the continent of Europe. Critics used to scorn this as cowardly practice by craven political organizations and as an example of the regimentation of American thought to such an extent that national elections were pointless. However, many will feel today that the dulness of past campaigns, revealing as it did little on which our people disagreed, was not to be despised. Political parties do not manufacture basic, disrupting issues. Rather are they inclined to dodge such issues as long as they can. When an issue has reached a stage in public opinion when it is to the profit of a party to take it up, the function of the leaders is to frame it in a form that will get votes. Even in war parties are apt to lag behind rather than to run ahead of public opinion. Their spirit of compromise and the internal discipline enforced within the organization are a harmonizing influence.

American habits being what they are, we shall attain greater unity through politics than by abandoning elections in favor of a semblance of national harmony. The United States entered the war divided on many issues and hampered by political animosities. The democracies which have fallen before Hitler were caught in even worse moments of weakness. If our war efforts to date have been retarded somewhat by tightly drawn lines of domestic issues, it is well to remember, nevertheless, that disputes concerning farm subsidies, price-fixing, labor unions, wage ceilings, and taxation can be resolved only as the people feel that their opinions are effective. We shall attain unity and preserve courage to surmount reverses only as each individual feels that he shares in the measures that are taken. Only through the substantial consent which arises from such sharing, and which no regimented opinion can supply, will we be given the endurance and resiliency we shall need. . . .

Although some believe that coalition government would be the best method to secure the unity and decisive action we need, conditions in the United States do not, I believe, promise success for this proposal. Since the United States has no experience with true coalition government and no tradition of it, with us a coalition would be apt to be merely a symbol of unity rather than a means of unity. One trouble today in certain administrative departments in Washington is that they contain men contending for differing programs and divergent policies. To the extent that administrative areas are in this condition, they are in fact suffering from a sort of coalition government. Undoubtedly this weakens an agency in its capacity to plan and execute coherent policies promptly. Since by definition a coalition is composed of men of differing political loyalties, it is bound to be weakened by internal struggles for power. It must rule by combination and compromise to a greater extent than a disciplined and smooth-running party organization.

England is the model always mentioned by advocates of coalition government for us. But the governmental system and traditions of the United States are quite different from England's. The President is in fact and in law the ceremonial head of the government, the master of his cabinet, and the leader of his party in Congress as well. His cabinet should be an extension of his personality and not a college of legislative leaders. On the other hand, the Prime Minister is not a chief executive in this wide American sense. While more than merely first among equals, he is yet the creature of Parliament and the cabinet. When the relations of the two heads towards their respective legislatures are considered, the differences between the two countries making for success or failure of leadership by coalition are obvious. Coalition government here would at best be a patriotic gesture purchased at too great cost. . . .

To work, coalition government must be coupled with a recess from elections. In the United States, however, we are by law and habit tied to fixed dates for elections. As already suggested, to omit an election would with us be a major operation. Within the limits beyond which the normal life of a Parliament cannot extend, English law and practice provide no fixed times for elections. Thus without threatening the popular basis of government or alarming public opinion, it was possible for the British parties to announce that there would be no general election during the war, even although the sitting Parliament had been elected as far back as 1935. . . .

If the foregoing analysis of the services rendered by political parties is correct, their responsibilities in these days are enormous. The government may freeze tires, but attempts to freeze opinion would be disastrous. It is too late to win this war by conditioning Americans to a one-party system. Our habits of criticism of public officials, our doctrine that they are always accountable to the people, are too deeply ingrained to be discarded, even in war, without violence to national solidarity and impairment of our military strength. We have available no methods of unity which do not involve the continued functioning of political parties.

21 ★ Albert Guérard, "A National Government?"

> *Republican gains in 1942 convinced some liberals that the continuation of party strife was too dangerous a luxury to afford. In a letter written to* The New Republic, *Albert Guérard set forth the argument for a national coalition government and expressed certain reservations about democratic processes in time of war.* [The New Republic, *LVIII (February 1, 1943), 150. Reprinted by permission of* The New Republic, © 1943, Harrison-Blaine of New Jersey, Inc.]

We all profess to believe that the war, and the peace for which we are waging war, are issues of such vital importance that they should be raised above the level of party politics. The natural consequence would be to form, as in Great Britain, a national government to meet the national emergency.

If, forgetting hoary conventions, we take a realistic view of the situation, we find, first of all, that we already have a coalition government of the British type, since two important Cabinet positions, as well as important ambassadorships, have been given to Republicans.

We find also that all effective action in this Congress will have in fact to be non-partisan. Democrats and Republicans are so evenly matched that there is no secure majority to carry out a strictly partisan program. No important measure can be passed without the consent of the opposition, which therefore must cease to be considered as an "opposition."

If we choose to retain the partisan labels, the Democrats, still nominally in power, are bound to suffer heavily, and, I submit, unjustly. For the Republicans will vote for all the essential war measures, and claim credit for their patriotism; but the Democrats alone will be blamed for the discomforts inevitably arising out of these measures. By 1944, we shall be fed up with restrictions and regulations. Our discontent, if it be allowed to take a political form, will lead to a reaction which may engulf the Democratic Party, the New Deal, and with them much of our recent social progress.

Again, if the administration remains nominally in the hands of the Democrats, the Republicans will be sorely tempted to make party capital out of any peace settlement that may be proposed: the one sacred principle in party politics being that the other side is inevitably wrong. Now, as President Roosevelt and Vice President Wallace are obviously committed to world organization, it is strictly possible that the Republicans may urge an immediate return to rugged individualism, *i.e.*, isolation or *sacro egoismo* in international affairs.

Unless—and the result would be hardly less dangerous—the Democrats should attempt to forestall such a move by favoring a peace settlement so cautious, so "realistic" that it could not be used against them at home. Such a compromise would of course be heartily welcome by the more conservative elements among our allies. Once more, the "starry-eyed boys" would be unceremoniously pushed aside. A wise peace settlement will require courage; and a party in fear of its rival cannot be courageous.

For all these reasons, I suggest that we keep the war and the peace out of politics; and as the war cannot be suspended, the proper way is to suspend party strife now.

There is nothing unrealistic about such a proposal. We are told that the bi-partisan system is essential to the proper working of free institutions. But England, Mother of Parliaments, has had coalition Cabinets for the last fifty years. The last war was waged, the present war is conducted, by such coalitions; and the cautious London Times urged that this method of government be continued over the transition and reconstruction periods. France won in 1914-18 because there was a Sacred Union, and fell in 1940 because there was none.

A coalition government is not an irresponsible autocracy. We are apt to confound the evil of partisan denigration ("smearing") with the stimulus of non-partisan criticism. I can hardly imagine Mr. Herbert Hoover or Mr. Wendell Willkie failing to speak out their minds, even though there should be two or three more Republicans in the national Cabinet.

We may be told that the bi-partisan system is with us a "sacred tradition." Perhaps we might remember that the Founders denounced parties, which they properly called *factions*.

When the present emergency is over, it may be desirable that party lines be drawn again. When this happens, let us trust it will be on intelligible lines—Standpatters v. Progressives; Opportunists v. Radicals—and not according to the present crazy pattern.

22 ★ Dwight Macdonald, "Why Politics?"

In February 1944, Dwight Macdonald founded Politics, *an avowedly Marxist magazine. The editor explained that the journal's "political tendency will be democratic socialist," and that it would "be partisan to those on the bottom of present-day society—the Negroes, the colonial peoples, and the vast majority of common people everywhere, including the Soviet Union." In the first issue, Macdonald explained why he thought the call for national unity had dangerous implications. [Politics, I (February, 1944), 6-8. Copyright 1944 by Politics. Reprinted by permission of Dwight Macdonald.]*

In common American usage, "politics" has either mean or invidious connotations. It suggests ward politics—graft, baby-kissing, petty chicanery. Or else an illegitimate putting forward of special interests at the expense of society as a whole, as when the press used to accuse Roosevelt of "playing politics" with unemployment relief. The word "politician" is practically a term of abuse.

This would seem to be a curious attitude. "Politics" to the Greeks, who were experts at it, had no such connotation. Webster defines the word in Aristotelian terms as "the science and art of government," which would seem unexceptionable enough. We can understand the bad odor of the word, however, if we consider the blunter contemporary definition: "who gets what, and how." The conception of "politics" thus appears to be something like "sex" or "profits," an overexplicit formulation of relationships polite bourgeois society prefers to keep hidden. It rends the fiction that all is harmonious and equitable within society. The bourgeois theory is that there is no necessity for politics, since the economic system distributes goods with Jovian impartiality, and every man has a chance to get precisely the amount of honor and possessions his individual qualifications entitle him to get. By definition, the interference of the politician must always be to pervert this self-adjusting system for the unfair benefit of some special interest. The ideal is, therefore, "A Businessman in the White House."

This objection to politics is pretty old-fashioned, and is vanishing along with the antiquated laisser-faire ideology it expressed. (The sad experience of the last "businessman in the White House," and the brilliant record of his super-political successor, helped along the demise of the conception—though it may be revived in future, anything being possible these days.) The modern attack on politics comes from another quarter: the ideal of national unity. In the United States at war, all respectable folk pay lip service to this ideal, and Roosevelt prefers the non-political role of Commander-in-Chief to the political one of President.

The National Committee of the American Communist Party, in recommending the party's dissolution, invoked the "national unity" concept, defining the future function of Communists as "to aid the struggle for the unity of the people in support of the nation's war policies, without partisan or class advantages." In the totalitarian nations politics has vanished completely, at least in the sense of open, institutionalized contests between various interest groups. There are no parties because there are no *parts*, only the whole, and there are no elections, except in form, because only one choice is, *even formally*, presented to the voter. (That different candidates compete against each other in Russian elections does not alter the picture, since all candidates have the same program and choice among them is, at best, a question of choice among their individual qualifications. Such elections might be called "administrative" rather than "political.") In Nazi propaganda the term "politician" is even more invidious than in American usage. In Soviet propaganda, it has disappeared completely; the very conception has been expunged from the consciousness of the Russian masses.

Thus "politics" is a most unpopular term in a world in which ever-thicker veils of official ideology swathe the brutal realities of power. Yet as long as class societies exist, the only hope of the submerged majority to change things in their favor will rest on political action, breaking through the fiction of organic unity between the lion and the lamb and setting class groups off openly against each other. In a classless society, of course, politics would cease to exist because it would have no further function. "We are very well off as to politics," says old Hammond in William Morris's *News from Nowhere*, "because we have none." The essence of reactionary politics is to try to get people to behave in a class society as though it were a classless society, i.e., to stop "playing politics."

Actually, by one of those dialectical turns so common in history, the more the anti-political concept of "national unity" gains, the wider the power of the State can be extended and the more thoroughly can all of society become politicalized. In the totalitarian countries, where politics is most severely repressed, all aspects of personal and cultural existence have become subject to political control. The same process is going on over here. It would therefore seem useful to have a magazine which, beginning with its very title, will constantly emphasize the political reality of anti-political ideology and practices.

. . . I think we can start out from the proposition that this war is not a struggle between Good and Evil, or Democracy and Totalitarianism, but rather a clash of rival imperialisms. This is now admitted much more widely in liberal-labor circles than it was at the beginning of the war. But to say it is an imperialist war does not exhaust the matter. For there certainly *are* important differences between fascism and democratic capitalism, and the outcome of the war certainly *does* "make a difference" to the workingclass in this country and elsewhere (including Germany). We of the Left cannot simply draw aside and say, it's none of our business, we don't care what happens.

From this, most of the Left, even those who agree as to the imperialist nature of the war, have drawn the conclusion that we must give support—"critical" support, of course—to the United Nations. Alexander Herzen remarks of two Russian liberals who made their peace with Czar Nicholas I: "I shall be told that under the aegis of devotion to the Imperial power, the truth can be spoken more boldly. Why, then, did they not speak it?" So, too, with the critical supporters of the war— why, then, do they not criticise? The difficulty is that the war, like the Czarist system, is a phenomenon of such historical weight that to accept it, with whatever reservations, means one is paralyzed on apparently secondary issues. One might imagine, for example, a policy of all support to the war effort combined with uncompromising struggle, through strikes and political action, for a progressive conduct of the war on the home front and in foreign policy. This is formally imaginable. Yet it is a historical impossibility, which is why the impact of the lib-labs on the conduct of this war has been so negligible. The interests of the present ruling classes of England and America cannot be reconciled with those of the masses in those countries, and so long as the war is conducted within the framework of the status quo, it cannot be wrenched around to serve the interests of a "people's century." This war has its own logic and its own drive, which the labor movement submits to in supporting it.

The proper policy would have been to insist on taking the fight against Hitler into the hands of the workers, to press for certain policies by means of strikes and political action regardless of the immediate effect on the war effort. This would have involved the risk of a Nazi victory? Of course. But risks are involved in any course, and the present policy of the Left does not even offer risks: it is leading straight to postwar reaction on a world scale, the redivision of Europe and the colonial regions between the three dominant imperialisms. The great aim of Roosevelt-Stalin-Churchill is to prevent "chaos" and "anarchy"—i.e., social revolution—in postwar Europe. But future hopes of progress will come out of "chaos," not out of "order."

It all comes down to: what are you interested in? If one is interested in basic social change, one weighs the risks and gains on one set of scales; if one is interested in buttressing the status quo as a "lesser evil," then one uses another set. . . . War is the supreme crisis of any class society; then as never in peacetime does the ruling class need the support of the ruled. Whether this crisis is seen as an *opportunity* or as a *danger* depends on where one's political interests lie.

THE WAR AND SOCIAL REFORM

The war affected reform in a variety of ways: it obviated the need for some reforms and set up obstacles to others, but it also helped revitalize the reform impulse. Clearly, wartime prosperity eliminated the need for certain New Deal projects designed to aid the unemployed. Moreover, even where reform was still in order the war erected certain barriers to it by subordinating social improvement to the requirements of victory. The necessity to check inflation precluded economic betterment for many workers whose wages had remained low, and the desire for maximum production undermined the Justice Department's antitrust program. Finally, the war attracted to government service members of a business elite possessed of managerial skill but little zeal for reform. While the war relegated reform to a back seat, it strengthened liberalism in some respects. By vastly increasing the scope of government regulation of the economy, the war weakened ideological resistance to federal control. Then too, because the war was being fought in the interest of the "common man," it was widely assumed that the veterans should not be allowed to return to a land scarred by joblessness, poverty, and insecurity.

23 ★ David E. Lilienthal, Social Gains in Wartime

At various times in 1942, David E. Lilienthal, chairman of the Tennessee Valley Authority, set down his thoughts on the relationship of the war to social reform. Lilienthal's comments indicated how the war tended to create a different order of priorities and establish new criteria by which reform would be judged. [From pp. 431-434, 543-545 *The Journals of David E. Lilienthal:* Volume I, The TVA Years, 1939-1945 by David E. Lilienthal. Copyright © 1964 by David E. Lilienthal. Reprinted by permission of Harper & Row, Publishers.]

JANUARY 14, 1942

I have been giving a good deal of thought in the last few months to this problem: To what extend can we hold, maintain, and even extend so-called social gains while we fight a war? Or, to put it another way, must we abandon or moderate social gains during such a war as this?

There is, of course, no single answer. I have evolved a kind of test that can be put this way: If the social gain is one that will further the war effort, then of course it should not be abandoned and might in fact be extended. If, however, it is in a sense a luxury, broadly speaking, something that will detract or diminish the effectiveness with which we carry on the war, then it should be regarded as "unfinished business" and either abandoned or curtailed.

There are two important points involved in this analysis, and neither of them is sufficiently well understood among the people I have talked to or listened to. First, progressives should understand that programs which do not forward the war must be given up or drastically curtailed. This is not an easy pill for many people to swallow. For one thing, some of our progressive friends have kept their zest for life at a boiling point because of fights with this or that predatory interest until they hardly have an interest in fighting Hitler.

I had an illustration of this the other night in talking to Governor Pinchot, an old battler against the corrupt utility machine of Pennsylvania and a conservationist of the pioneer variety—a grand old man, too. He was a little disappointed when in response to a question from him I said I didn't think the fight against public utility excesses was currently of much consequence. From a human point of view, it is easy to understand the letdown that comes when issues that you have lived on for so long are no longer important.

The REA program is another illustration. Some of the men who have given a great deal to that enterprise, both in Congress and in the agency itself, are carrying on as if we were not in a war and as if the battle were still one of spite lines, etc. A good deal of . . . trouble during the past few months—not all of it, but a good deal of it—has come because the REA people were definitely more interested in copper for farm lines than for shells and airplane motors—not if the issue were sharply put that way, of course, but at bottom that was precisely the trouble.

Now I have as good a right to offer myself as an exponent of farm electrification as anybody, and I know all about the fights that are so often involved. And I know, too, that farm electrification in a long-range sense is a means of fortifying the country's morale, and that is a matter of first importance. But since farm electrification by simple arithmetic means taking copper in large quantities away from the Army and the

Navy that need it badly, and since it means motors, electric refrigerators, etc., that use materials that we need for this fight, it doesn't seem to me there is any need for fine-spun arguments showing that farmers with electricity on their farms produce more food, and an Army needs food, etc. Farm electrification on any important scale at the moment comes under the heading of "unfinished business."

And of course the same thing applies in the expansion of consumer use of electricity. This is a highly desirable social gain, and we have accomplished it to a degree in the Tennessee Valley, but with electricity sorely needed for war production, that too comes under the heading of unfinished business, to be resumed when this mess is all over. . . .

A lot of rabid reactionaries and even many honest conservatives feel that this is the time to get rid of the newfangled social legislation enacted since 1933 and even prior thereto. They argue that it was the seven-hour day for labor organizations that ruined France, and Willkie had a good deal of that in his campaign speeches. Therefore, there is a strong effort to liquidate a good many of these social gains for the duration of the war.

But the fact of the business is that many of these social changes actually further the war effort. Collective bargaining is a good example. Collective bargaining and good labor-management working arrangements are as much a measure for the successful prosecution of the war as having first-class tools in the factories. We have found that not only is it a protection against interruption of work, but on the affirmative side, it actually promotes speed and efficiency and, as few people recognize, is an effective method of detecting and combating sabotage. Immediately after our 15-union contract was signed, the Tennessee Valley Trades and Labor Council passed a resolution pledging continuity for defense production (this was in September of 1940) *and* very specifically referring to sabotage. It is well known that the detection of industrial sabotage is a most difficult and expensive thing. To have an organization of workers each of whom regards it as part of his responsibility to take care lest sabotage occur is probably a very considerable protection.

And so collective bargaining under the principles laid down by the Wagner Act as a national policy and as we set it out in TVA's labor policy back in 1934 is unquestionably a social gain that, far from being sacrificed, should be fortified and continued.

I asked the question about maintenance of social gains of Lewis Mumford the other night. His answer was that to the extent that social gains meant luxuries and doodads for a part of the population, they would have to be dispensed with and that we were just starting to see the beginning of that. But to that large part of the population that had had a standard of living, even as to food, below the level at which men can be vigorous, normal animals and continue their work, those social gains would have to be extended and expanded if we are to do the job.

Each morning I have a visual demonstration of how true this is. The Tennessee Employment Agency's office is on the way from where I park my car to my office, and usually lined up outside is quite a queue of men and sometimes women making application for work. Across the street is the draft board office, and there is not infrequently a line of men outside that office. You don't have to be a nutritionist or doctor to see that at least half these folks are miserably undernourished, even the young people being stooped, sallow, and badly in need of dental care, etc. This is after almost nine years of "prosperity" as compared to the "depression" period! . . .

SEPTEMBER 29, 1942

. . . The men in the fighting forces and the men in defense industries, perhaps farmers as well, ought to have soon a specific assurance that the country will be ready with a vigorous dynamic program of expansion after the war, a program in which every able-bodied, decent person will have a chance. There is nothing impossible about that unless we doubt it. All it takes is the faint shadow of a doubt to start a reverse cycle that will destroy the possibility of any such momentum. These things are highly intangible and subtle. Generalized talk won't do it, and too much oratory about this being a people's war, etc., is going to work out badly, too.

Contrary to my earlier notions about it, it seems to me this sort of a program is part of the winning of the war. A soldier's first thought when he isn't in actual combat is getting it *over* and getting back home. Don't tell me that it will not be the greatest possible strengthening of morale, fighting morale, for ten million men to feel that when they do get it over they are coming back to a country that is ready to go into high gear with a chance for every one of them to apply the things they have learned in the Army to civilian life.

It's too early to be sure, and there are many factors, of course, but I am sure that the Russian fighting spirit must be closely related to the enormous pride the Russians have in their expansion program and their desire to resume it. The Russians, as a Tank Corps song I heard the other night indicates, don't glorify war as an end in itself; it is a bloody mess to be gotten over with so they can go back and build more tractor factories.

If we can recapture the spirit of expansion, and really let ourselves go in that direction, we will then have a central driving force, a sense of security rather than of frustration. And such a feeling is essential after hostilities if we are to take responsibility in world affairs. A man who is unsteady, unsure, and full of fears about himself is not going to be much interested in helping in community affairs. And it is going to be just too easy for the America Firsters, who are dormant but not dead, to make a killing with their story if the country is in the doldrums economically when this is over and has no vigorous plan to snap out of it.

24 ★ *Malcolm Cowley,* "The End of the New Deal"

> *By the middle of 1943, a common complaint among liberals was that the New Deal was dying and that its spokesmen were powerless. One reformer, for example, grumbled that "the New Dealers are a vanishing tribe, and the money-changers who were driven from the temple are now quietly established in government offices." In the following essay, Malcolm Cowley argued that the President's reform program had been jettisoned and suggested what might be the result. [The New Republic, CVIII (May 31, 1943), 729-32. Reprinted by permission of the magazine and the author.]*

There is a story from Washington that is bigger than all the other stories about the home front. It is so big that, although often mentioned in passing, it has never been treated as a whole; and yet most of the other big and little stories depend on it. . . . Briefly, the story is that the New Deal is being abandoned, and perhaps for a long time; that the New Dealers are losing their government posts and that a new crowd is preparing to take over. It is a change somewhat slower than the one that took place in 1933, after Roosevelt's first inauguration, but it promises to be almost as sweeping.

Already it is possible to compile a long casualty list of New Deal agencies that have been killed or crippled since 1941. The Civilian Conservation Corps was the first to go; it was abolished by Congress. The Work Projects Administration was given what the President called an "honorable discharge." The Farm Security Administration will cease to exist at the end of the fiscal year, unless the agricultural-appropriations bill is rewritten by the Senate. The Home Owners' Loan Corporation was condemned to quick death by a House amendment, but the Senate wants to grant a stay of execution, so that its assets can be liquidated "in an orderly manner." The National Resources Planning Board, which the House wants to abolish overnight, may also be reprieved by the Senate, but at best it will linger on as an advisory committee without power and almost without funds. The choice is between lynching and confinement to an asylum. Even the Securities and Exchange Commission is being granted so little money that it will have a hard time protecting investors during the new era of speculation now getting under way.

The National Labor Relations Board, charged with administering the Wagner Act, has little to do at present and is uncertain about its own future. Many members of its staff are in the army or are working for the war agencies, on loan. The National Youth Administration is limited to a training program for young people about to enter war industries. The Rural Electrification Administration, with a greatly reduced budget, is being investigated by the Cannon Committee, and not in any friendly spirit. The Federal Communications Commission is being investigated by its sworn enemy, Representative Cox of Georgia. The Tennessee Valley Authority has been popular and extremely effective, but it would fall under political control if the McKellar bill was passed. The only agencies to escape being attacked are so obscure or inactive that Congress has overlooked them.

It is true that some of the work performed by New Deal agencies had become unnecessary under changed conditions. For example, with full employment there is no need for work projects—although in retrospect it seems pretty foolish to have swept out the WPA like trash from the attic, without reflecting that its experience would be useful in meeting the severe unemployment problems we are likely to face after the war. With boys of eighteen in the army, there is no present need for CCC camps. On the other hand, many of the New Deal activities are or would be far more useful in wartime than they were during the depression. Housing, public health, recreational facilities, maternity care, day nurseries for the children of working mothers, loans and advice for small farmers, camps for migratory workers, crop control—all these are essential parts of the manpower program or the food program, or both. Either they are being abandoned for want of appropriations, or else they are being carried out timidly and ineffectually in order to escape the attention of the hatchetmen in Congress. . . .

People in Washington thought for a time that the most needed community services of the New Deal might be continued during the war by the Office of Civilian Defense, with the help of volunteer workers, and by the Office of Defense Health and Welfare Services. Both offices set to work on ambitious paper programs. But OCD had to drop these activities after the congressional uproar over the "fan dancer";* and the other office, which never became famous enough to be known by its initials, has either been very discreet or almost completely inactive. Nobody regards the army or the navy as New Deal agencies, but nevertheless they are responsible for the health and morale of their men. They happen to be almost the only departments that have been carrying on a certain amount of new welfare work, including the only large-scale adult-education programs and the only government-sponsored art projects now in operation.

Most of the important wartime agencies are being run by conservatives—often conservative Republicans—or by "practical" men borrowed from business life. That is true of the Food Administration, the Rubber Administration, the Maritime Commission and the War Production Board. At the Office of Price Administration, Prentiss Brown has been trying to keep prices down without offending anybody, with the result that nobody is satisfied and his own staff is in revolt. Many of the skilled executives whom he inherited from Leon Henderson have left or will soon be leaving. The War Manpower Commission has shown a tendency to give management more weight than labor; at least that is what friends of Deputy Chairman Harper said in explaining his resignation. The Fair Employment Practice Committee of WMC, which had been fighting racial discrimination, has lately been kept from fighting anything. The Office of War Information has been watering down its reports, so as not to offend Congress. Gardner Cowles, a newspaper publisher and a Republican, is head of its domestic branch, from which many New Dealers have been resigning. The Board of Economic Warfare, under Vice President Wallace and Milo Perkins, has more New Dealers on its staff than any other of the war agencies, but recently its polices have been timorous and conservative. Harold L. Ickes, as Fuel Administrator, seems to be following his own stubbornly courageous path—but then he never got along too badly with business men.

Most of the New Dealers yielded more easily than anyone expected. Some of those who resigned from their jobs as a protest might have

* EDITOR'S NOTE: A Congressional furor developed when Mrs. Franklin D. Roosevelt, as head of the Volunteer Participation Committee of the Office of Civilian Defence, invited the night club dancer Mayris Chaney to direct part of the agency's physical fitness program. Congressmen of both parties attacked the employment by the government of an alleged "fan dancer," and in February 1942 the House censured such employment. Soon after, Mrs. Roosevelt and Miss Chaney resigned, as did OCD Director Fiorello H. La Guardia.

stayed to fight for their principles. Others resigned from their principles instead, as a means of keeping their jobs—and usually ended by losing the jobs also. There are some pretty unpleasant stories of executives who changed their policies and dismissed their subordinates so as not to offend congressmen with a grudge. Each agency under attack was left to struggle alone; apparently the others thought that if WPA or Farm Security or the National Youth Administration was sacrificed to Congress, the others could continue their work undisturbed. It was like throwing babies to the wolves, but the pack never stopped.

It is not hard to understand why many of the New Dealers failed to act boldly. They had been trained and hired to do a job rather than to fight a political battle. After Pearl Harbor, the President seemed to lose interest in their work, and they no longer had the support of the labor unions. It was difficult for them to follow a determined policy without support from below or direction from above. They must have felt like men halfway up a cliff, when the ledge on which they are standing breaks away and the rope by which they are held is suddenly released. Some of them, like Leon Henderson in the past, and now James L. Fly and Clifford J. Durr of the Federal Communications Commission, have been putting up a brave fight without much backing. In general the brave, the timid, the able administrators and the windbags have all been sacrificed together. . . .

What has happened in Washington since Pearl Harbor is the defeat of a whole class of people who went to work for the government, not in the expectation of becoming rich or powerful—though some of them learned to love power—and not in the hope of building up estates that would provide safe incomes for their children, but simply because they wanted to have fruitful careers and get things done. They hoped to be the engineers of American prosperity. Their principal economic ambition for themselves—it will never be realized—was not having to worry about bills. They are the people who are interested in ideas and are not frightened by new ones. Instead of playing bridge, they talk about America, Russia, France, England; and they read books—a student of folkways could learn a great deal by studying the sales records of the Washington bookstores for the last twenty years. As a class, they are good at making programs, fairly good as administrators, and very poor as rough-and-tumble politicians. . . .

I have heard people surmising that even in Washington the fortunes of war might change. They say that Roosevelt, early in 1944, might reappoint New Dealers to office and might resume his liberal policies in order to carry the fall elections. But such a course might prove to be politically inadvisable, since it would merely confuse the public at large. More than that, it would be politically impossible with the present Congress in its present mood. The liberal policies wouldn't be supported by appropriations. The New Dealers would either have to resign under pressure, or else Congress would abolish their agencies. . . .

When a dollar-a-year man tells you late at night that maybe Hitler had the right idea—"But get me straight, we've got to lick him first"— and when an army officer says, "We'll have to kick out all those long-hairs and set up a business government. Just wait till the boys get home" —at such moments you reflect unhappily that the United States Government is a vast machine that could be used for other purposes besides national defense and furthering the common welfare. Perhaps you also reflect that the Nazis created their new German empire without making many changes in the German bureaucracy. For example, the Ministry of Justice had in 1939 exactly the same higher personnel that it had in 1932, before Hitler. Franz Neumann says in "Behemoth" that a law expelling non-Aryans and other "unreliable elements" from the civil service led to the dismissal of only 211 career officials in Prussia, and the demotion or transfer of 258. In the other states of the Reich, 1.13 per cent of the higher civil servants were discharged and 2.33 per cent were transferred —and with these changes the state machine belonged to the Nazis. It is possible that a fascist state could be instituted here without many changes in government personnel, and some of those changes have been made already.

THE ELECTION OF 1944

The Presidential campaign of 1944 was particularly rancorous, even though the candidates were not far apart on major issues. While President Roosevelt campaigned less vigorously than in the past, he delivered several brilliant speeches pledging to extend the liberal program after the war and provide leadership in the search for peace. The hopes of the Republican candidate, Thomas E. Dewey, rested on his belief that voters had become fatigued with wartime controls and resentful of left-wing influence in the Administration. Dewey's promise to preserve New Deal social advances and pursue a policy of internationalism marked an important advance in bipartisan acceptance of the essential features of the Rooseveltian program. The contest was apparently decided by the voters' reluctance to change leadership in a time of crisis, Dewey's inability to stake out an independent position, and overwhelming support for Roosevelt in the cities. Roosevelt received 25.6 million votes to his opponent's 22 million, and the Democrats increased their margin of control in Congress.

25 ★ *Franklin D. Roosevelt,* An Economic Bill of Rights

> *Roosevelt's State of the Union message in January, 1944 contained his most elaborate statement of the reform ideology. The United States, he said, was determined not to repeat the errors of "ostrich isolationism" or "the excesses of the wild twenties when this Nation went for a joy ride on a roller coaster which ended in a tragic crash." He also called for the subordination of "individual or group selfishness to the national good" through a high tax on corporate profits, continued price stabilization, and national service. The speech served as the basis for his 1944 campaign.* [Samuel I. Rosenman, ed., *The Public Papers and Addresses of Franklin D. Roosevelt* (New York: Harper and Bros., 1950), XIII, 40-42. Reprinted by permission.]

The overwhelming majority of our people have met the demands of this war with magnificent courage and understanding. They have accepted inconveniences; they have accepted hardships; they have accepted tragic sacrifices. And they are ready and eager to make whatever further contributions are needed to win the war as quickly as possible— if only they are given the chance to know what is required of them.

However, while the majority goes on about its great work without complaint, a noisy minority maintains an uproar of demands for special favors for special groups. There are pests who swarm through the lobbies of the Congress and the cocktail bars of Washington, representing these special groups as opposed to the basic interests of the Nation as a whole. They have come to look upon the war primarily as a chance to make profits for themselves at the expense of their neighbors—profits in money or in terms of political or social preferment.

Such selfish agitation can be highly dangerous in wartime. It creates confusion. It damages morale. It hampers our national effort. It muddies the waters and therefore prolongs the war. . . .

It is our duty now to begin to lay the plans and determine the strategy for the winning of a lasting peace and the establishment of an American standard of living higher than ever before known. We cannot be content, no matter how high that general standard of living may be, if some fraction of our people—whether it be one-third or one-fifth or one-tenth—is ill-fed, ill-clothed, ill-housed, and insecure.

This Republic had its beginning, and grew to its present strength, under the protection of certain inalienable political rights—among them the right of free speech, free press, free worship, trial by jury, freedom from unreasonable searches and seizures. They were our rights to life and liberty.

As our Nation has grown in size and stature, however—as our industrial economy expanded—these political rights proved inadequate to assure us equality in the pursuit of happiness.

We have come to a clear realization of the fact that true individual freedom cannot exist without economic security and independence. "Necessitous men are not free men." People who are hungry and out of a job are the stuff of which dictatorships are made.

In our day these economic truths have become accepted as self-evident. We have accepted, so to speak, a second Bill of Rights under which a new basis of security and prosperity can be established for all —regardless of station, race, or creed.

Among these are:

The right to a useful and remunerative job in the industries or shops or farms or mines of the Nation;

The right to earn enough to provide adequate food and clothing and recreation;

The right of every farmer to raise and sell his products at a return which will give him and his family a decent living;

The right of every businessman, large and small, to trade in an atmosphere of freedom from unfair competition and domination by monopolies at home or abroad;

The right of every family to a decent home;

The right to adequate medical care and the opportunity to achieve and enjoy good health;

The right to adequate protection from the economic fears of old age, sickness, accident, and unemployment;

The right to a good education.

All of these rights spell security. And after this war is won we must be prepared to move forward, in the implementation of these rights, to new goals of human happiness and well-being.

America's own rightful place in the world depends in large part upon how fully these and similar rights have been carried into practice for our citizens. For unless there is security here at home there cannot be lasting peace in the world.

One of the great American industrialists of our day—a man who has rendered yeoman service to his country in this crisis—recently emphasized the grave dangers of "rightist reaction" in this Nation. All clear-thinking businessmen share his concern. Indeed, if such reaction should develop—if history were to repeat itself and we were to return to the so-called "normalcy" of the 1920's—then it is certain that even though we shall have conquered our enemies on the battlefields abroad, we shall have yielded to the spirit of Fascism here at home.

I ask the Congress to explore the means for implementing this economic bill of rights—for it is definitely the responsibility of the Congress so to do. Many of these problems are already before committees of the Congress in the form of proposed legislation. I shall from time to time communicate with the Congress with respect to these and further proposals. In the event that no adequate program of progress is evolved, I am certain that the Nation will be conscious of the fact.

Our fighting men abroad—and their families at home—expect such a program and have the right to insist upon it. It is to their demands that this Government should pay heed rather than to the whining demands of selfish pressure groups who seek to feather their nests while young Americans are dying.

26 ★ *Thomas E. Dewey*, Campaign Address

The speech with which Dewey opened his campaign in September, 1944, introduced the major issues he exploited in the months that followed. Another theme emerged a few days later when Dewey declared that labor "racketeers and the Communists are against a change of administration." [Congressional Record, 78th Cong., 2nd Sess., LXXXX, Part 11, A3988-89.]

At the very outset I want to make one thing clear. This is not merely a campaign against an individual or a political party. It is not merely a campaign to displace a tired, exhausted, quarreling and bickering administration with a fresh and vigorous administration.

It is a campaign against an administration which was conceived in defeatism, which failed for eight straight years to restore our domestic economy, which has been the most wasteful, extravagant and incompetent administration in the history of the Nation and, worst of all, one which has lost faith in itself and in the American people. . . .

When this administration took office the depression was already over 3 years old. Then what happened? In 1934, when the depression was then 5 years old—longer than any other in a century, we still had 12,000,-000 unemployed. By 1940 the depression was almost 11 years old. This administration had been in power for 7 straight years and there were still 10,000,000 Americans unemployed.

It took a world war to get jobs for the American people.

Let's get one thing clear and settled. Who was President during the depression that lasted from 1933 until some time in 1940, when war orders from all over the world began to bring us full employment again? The New Deal kept this country in a continuous state of depression for 7 straight years. It made a 3-year depression last 11 years—over twice as long as any other depression in a whole century.

Now, Washington is getting all set for another depression. They intend to keep the young men in the Army. The New Deal spokesmen are daily announcing that reconversion will be difficult, if not impossible. They say that relief rolls will be enormous. They drearily promise us that we shall need to prepare for an army of unemployed bigger than the armies we have put in the field against the Germans and the Japanese. That's what's wrong with the New Deal. That's why it's time for a change.

The reason for this long-continued failure is twofold. First, because there never was a worse job done of running our Government. When one agency fails, the New Deal just piles another on and we pay for both. When men quarrel, there is no one in authority to put a stop to it. When agencies get snarled up there is no one in authority to untangle them. Meanwhile, the people's business goes to pot and the people are the victims. . . .

The other reason for this long continued failure—the reason why they are now dismally preparing for another depression—is because this administration has so little faith in the United States. They believe in the defeatist philosophy that our industrial plant is built, that our task is not to produce more goods but to fight among ourselves over what we have.

I believe that we have not even begun to build our industrial plant. We have not exhausted our inventive genius. We have not exhausted our capacity to produce more goods for our people. No living man has yet dreamed of the limit to which we can go if we have a Government which believes in the American economic system and in the American people. . . .

The war has proved that despite the New Deal, America can mightily increase its frontiers of production. With competent government America can produce mightily for peace. And the standard of living of our people is limited only by the amount of goods and services we are able to produce. . . .

We know from long experience that we shall not provide jobs and restore small business by the methods of the New Deal. We cannot keep our freedom and at the same time continue experimentation with a new policy every day by the National Government. We cannot succeed with a controlled and regulated society under a Government which destroys incentive, chokes production, fosters disunity and discourages men with vision and imagination from creating employment and opportunity.

The New Deal really believes that unemployment is bound to be with us permanently. It says so. They will change this 12-year-old tune between now and election. They have done it every time. But they've always come back to it after election. The New Deal really believes that we cannot have good social legislation and also good jobs for all. I believe with all my heart and soul that we can have both.

Of course we need security regulation. Of course we need bank deposit insurance. Of course we need price support for agriculture. Of course the farmers of this country cannot be left to the hazards of a world price while they buy their goods at an American price. Of course we need unemployment insurance and old-age pensions and also relief whenever there are not enough jobs. Of course the rights of labor to organize and bargain collectively are fundamental. My party blazed the trail in that field by passage of the Railway Labor Act in 1926.

But we must also have a Government which believes in enterprise and Government policies which encourage enterprise. We must see to it that a man who wants to start a business is encouraged to start it, that the man who wants to expand a going business is encouraged to expand it. We must see to it that the job-producing enterprises of America are stimulated to produce more jobs. We must see to it that the man who wants to produce more jobs is not throttled by the Government—but knows that he has a Government as eager for him to succeed as he is himself.

We cannot have jobs and opportunity if we surrender our freedom to Government control. We do not need to surrender our freedom to Government control in order to have the economic security to which we are entitled as freemen. We can have both opportunity and security within the framework of a free society. That is what the American people will say at the election next November.

4 Civil Liberties and Civil Rights

TOLERANCE VERSUS CONFORMITY
World War II brought less pressure for conformity and fewer restrictions upon civil liberties than were anticipated. Both President Roosevelt and Attorney General Francis Biddle had libertarian inclinations. More important, the absence of widespread opposition to the war and the voluntary acceptance of censorship diminished the need for suppression. The nature of the war also tended to curb tendencies toward vigilante action, for it was being fought against an enemy identified with brutality and violence. Finally, twenty years after the enactment of immigration restriction, the United States seemed less vulnerable to dangers that might result from divided loyalties. But the balance between restraint and intolerance was tenuous. The war unleashed widespread animosity toward citizens of Japanese descent, led to serious outbreaks of racial violence directed at Negroes and Mexican-Americans, and apparently coincided with an increase in anti-Semitism. Civil liberties received far greater protection than during the First World War, but the record was by no means unblemished.

27 ★ American Civil Liberties Union, "Freedom in Wartime"

The American Civil Liberties Union, under the leadership of Roger N. Baldwin, had struggled for nearly twenty-five years against infringements upon freedom of expression. In 1942, the organization decided not to participate in civil liberties cases involving defendants who seemed to be "co-operating with or acting on behalf of the enemy," unless "the fundamentals of due process are denied." In June, 1943, the ACLU surveyed the state of civil liberties at the midpoint of the war. ["Freedom in Wartime," Report of the American Civil Liberties Union (June 1943), 3-6. Reprinted by permission.]

The striking contrast between the state of civil liberty in the first eighteen months of World War II and in World War I offers strong evidence to support the thesis that our democracy can fight even the greatest of all wars and still maintain the essentials of liberty. The country in World War II is almost wholly free of those pressures which in the first World War resulted in mob violence against dissenters, hundreds of prosecutions for utterances; in the creation of a universal volunteer vigilante system, officially recognized, to report dissent to the F.B.I.; in hysterical hatred of everything German; in savage sentences for private expressions of criticism; and in suppression of public debate of the issues of the war and the peace.

No such atmosphere marks the present war. We experience no hysteria, no war-inspired mob violence, no pressure for suppressing dissent, no activity of a secret political police, no organization of virtuous patriots seeking out seditious opinion, and no hostility to persons of German or Italian origin. Hostility to persons of Japanese ancestry, while painfully in evidence, is largely confined to the Pacific Coast and smaller communities in the west.

The government has not resorted to prosecution or censorship on any appreciable scale. War-time prosecutions brought by the Department of Justice for utterances, and publications barred by the Post Office Department as obstructive, have so far numbered about forty-five, involving less than two hundred persons, compared with over a thousand persons involved in almost as many cases in World War I. Even though some of the proceedings were hardly justified by any reasonable interpretation of the "clear and present danger" test laid down by the Supreme Court, the Department of Justice has on the whole shown commendable restraint.

A striking test of our progress in war-time tolerance is the much more favorable attitude to Jehovah's Witnesses, whose anti-war propaganda and public activities are calculated to provoke patriotic opposition. Yet in contrast with World War I, when their leaders were jailed and their propaganda curbed, and with outbursts against them in 1940, they have been accorded by the courts and by public opinion even greater liberties than in time of peace.

Conclusions as to our comparative freedom are supported not only by observation of the larger national aspects, but by local observers all over the country. A check-up early in 1943 with 112 correspondents of the Union in 41 states showed remarkable unanimity on the almost complete absence of repressive tendencies, and a surprising freedom of debate and criticism of war measures. Many of them reported the general climate of freedom in their localities as much better than even a year ago.

The record of violations of civil liberties shows the extraordinary fact that more issues and cases have arisen from the normal conflicts in our democracy than from the pressures of war, though some have been accentuated by war-time strains. In that continuing field, the record, particularly in May and June with the agitation over the miners' strikes and the outbreaks of racial mob violence, has been far from encouraging.

The causes of the heartening contrast with World War I in war-inspired issues are to be found in the comparatively slight opposition to the war,—concealed and unorganized,—against a vigorous radical and pacifist opposition then; in the widespread opposition to the Administration from powerful sources acting in the conventional democratic pattern, which tends to keep open the channels of debate and criticism; in the concentration of public attention not on attitudes to the war but on the debate as to what kind of a post-war world we are in process of creating; in the liberal policies of the Administration; and in the much firmer foundations put under the Bill of Rights in the last decade by numerous Supreme Court decisions.

The measures taken by the government to intern dangerous enemy aliens, to denaturalize the disloyal who acquired citizenship by fraud, to control espionage and sabotage,—virtually nonexistent,—the centralization of controls in Washington, have all tended to allay fear and to create the conviction that any movements obstructive of the war are well in hand.

But this encouraging war record is not without its inevitable exceptions. From the viewpoint of both the numbers affected and the seriousness of the rights violated, undoubtedly the worst single invasion of citizens' liberties under war pressures was the wholesale evacuation from the Pacific Coast of over 70,000 Americans of Japanese ancestry and their subsequent confinement in what are virtually concentration camps. The evils and injustices of that desperate move, dictated by race prejudice and military precaution, have been somewhat relieved by permitting those found to be loyal to leave the centers and resettle outside the military zones; by recently accepting into the army volunteers of Japanese ancestry after excluding them from Selective Service, and even by permitting soldiers in uniform to return to the evacuated area. But none of the measures are yet nearly adequate to restore the rights of American citizens nor to offer a long-range solution. Despite the Supreme Court's decision that the restrictions were constitutionally justified in a war emergency, the practical problem will long remain of repairing the vast damage done, materially and morally, to a helpless minority of our fellow-citizens,—and to our own democracy.

The same emergency powers invoked to evacuate the Japanese permitted the military to remove individual citizens from zones where their presence was regarded as dangerous to military security,—an unprecedented power exercised by star-chamber proceedings before military commissions, but sparingly used, and resulting as yet in the removal of only a small number of people, and with only two court contests of the military power, both pending.

In the larger arena of communication an exception to the excellent record of war-time control of press and radio under voluntary codes must be recorded in the censorship of non-military news cabled to allied nations. Undue caution as to what news and opinion might feed the Axis propaganda machine has led to unreasonable restraints, particularly on news of race conflicts, and to frequent complaints by foreign correspondents.

The treatment of conscientious objectors, so much better in principle than in World War I, has nevertheless resulted in imprisoning more than three times as many, in large part because of a narrow interpretation of "religious training and belief" and reluctance to parole men to useful occupations. The administration of the Selective Service law has resulted in jailing hundreds of Jehovah's Witnesses, who demand a status as ministers although they are not employed full-time in that occupation and who, when that status is denied, prefer jail to any form of compulsory war service. The Supreme Court has, however, agreed to review one case in which draft boards denied the ministerial status. More Jehovah's Witnesses are in prison today for their particular brand of conscience than any other minority in the country.

Although the government has generously freed all Italian enemy aliens of war-time restrictions, it has not yet moved to free a class with an even greater claim on our democracy—the anti-Nazi German refugees who are still under the same restrictions as apply to all enemy aliens.

In addition to these exceptions to the generally favorable administration of war-time controls, apprehension is expressed in many quarters over the effects on our liberties of the vastly expanded war-time powers of government. Many, indeed, profess to see in measures already taken the outlines of a totalitarian state. But these measures largely concern economic controls which do not directly affect freedom of opinion and debate, nor the right of opposition or of criticism. Apprehension is also expressed over the prospects of the passage of a civilian compulsory war-service act, and its presumed effects in regimenting the entire population. But fear for the future of our democracy does not negate the plain facts of a record so far generally encouraging.

28 ★ *Norman Thomas, "War and Freedom"*

> *Socialist leader Norman Thomas, who had opposed American intervention during the 1930's, supported the war after the attack on Pearl Harbor. Nevertheless, he suspected that the war would erode traditional freedoms and offered a rejoinder to those civil libertarians who, he believed, were unduly optimistic.* [Common Sense, *XII (May 1943), 156-59. Reprinted by permission of Norman Thomas.*]

Americans concerned for the future can find little cause for optimism in the political situation here or abroad. Despite more favorable military prospects than anyone could have expected last summer, the outlook for a just peace grows worse.

It is therefore with a double satisfaction that most liberals contemplate what they believe to be the flourishing state of American civil liberty, even in the midst of total war. Though our freedoms have more than once been in jeopardy since Pearl Harbor, instances of suppression have been exceptional rather than general, and at present things seem to be getting better instead of worse. So happy a situation would seem to be not only good in itself, but to give promise of freedom for the discussion of the difficult problems that lie ahead. But let's look at the record.

Now it is true that there has been almost no interference by legal authorities or by mobs with public meetings. There has been no interference with the press comparable to what happened in the first World War, and no parallel to the wholesale arrests under the Espionage Act. Snoopers, official and unofficial, do not haunt every meeting as they did twenty-five years ago. In that war, the unpopular sect, Jehovah's Witnesses, was the object of systematic prosecution for sedition. Nothing of the sort has happened during this war; mob violence against the sect, widespread during 1940, has abated, partly as a result of vigorous action by the federal government. . . .

Of the treatment of conscientious objectors and pacifists, the optimists can say, with some justification, that our record, though not as good as England's, and far short of ideal, is at least better than in the last war. There has been no mob violence against pacifists. For religious believers, service under civilian control is formally recognized in the Selective Service Law as an alternative to military service. In interpreting this law different draft boards have adopted very different standards, and no adequate alternative service has been recognized. . . .

Meanwhile, more than 1500 conscientious objectors are in jail—two or three times the number in the first World War—because various draft boards did not recognize their objections as arising from "religious training and belief," or because they felt they could not accept the alternatives offered to military service, or because they refused to make even the gesture of compliance involved in registration. Many pacifists are there ready, even eager, to perform useful, disagreeable, or dangerous jobs for society at home or abroad. On the whole, however, objectors in this war have done less to advance the principle of freedom of conscience than they did in the first World War under more confused and often rougher conditions. Public indifference and official tolerance have lulled those concerned with civil liberties into complacence.

Why then, should we not accept with thankful hearts the optimist's view of the sound state of civil liberties? For two principal reasons.

First, the optimist greatly exaggerates the role of a determined and intelligent love of freedom by the people and the government in creating the present situation. This love does exist. But it is not very much stronger than that which existed in the first World War, as the optimist asserts. The present situation, in so far as it is really favorable, is mostly an accident, a by-product of certain historical events. The most important of these has no precedent in American history. In every previous war in which we have engaged there has been organized political opposition of varying strength. Last time, despite rigorous suppression, opposition was persistent and by no means confined to enemy sympathizers. Opposition to active participation in this war, strong before Pearl Harbor, completely dissolved after the surprise attack by Japan and the Japanese and German declarations of war against the United States. However unhappy millions of Americans may have felt about the war, they saw no political answer to it and no desirable peace, at least until the power of the enemy to dictate terms to the world was destroyed. . . .

If more stupid men had held high office in the Department of Justice, they might have missed the obvious point that, in a country with no significant political opposition to the war, persecution would boomerang. Attorney General Biddle and his associates are not stupid men, and their original bias was liberal. Another factor was the public confidence in the FBI, and hence, thanks partly to that and partly to community sentiment, the amazing lack of sabotage in America.

For these reasons there has been comparative freedom for discussion of the war and its issues. At the same time, it is important to observe that newspapers, publishers, and radio stations, consciously or unconsciously, exercise the kind of restraints which save the government the trouble of cracking down. It is far harder than the average man knows to bring before the public any adequate presentation of some aspects of labor problems, or race relations, or certain points of view regarding the peace. . . .

I analyze these unconscious and accidental factors making for comparative freedom in order to check the dangerous overconfidence of the optimists in our virtue. But there is a much weightier reason to challenge the optimists. In a very fundamental respect freedom is far more dangerously menaced in this war than in the last one.

This is because the Fascist-Nazi threat did not exist in 1917-18. By threat I do not mean simply the threat of world conquest held over our heads by the Axis, but the internal threat. The totalitarian glorification of the state, particularly the national or racial state, the belief that the state can do no wrong and that the individual is of no account before it, these attitudes have been growing in all modern states. Even those states longest democratic have, under modern social and economic pressures, shown this tendency. Total war necessarily strengthens it. This subtle, almost unconscious process, by which our minds become habituated to totalitarian methods, that presents the greatest danger to our liberties. It is my second and strongest reason for challenging the optimists.

Consider the power assumed by the President in his executive order of February 19, 1942, to evacuate American citizens, against whom no charges of any sort had been brought, from their homes and businesses, and to intern them for an indefinite period in lonely barrack cities behind barbed wire. This was done to more than seventy thousand American citizens of Japanese ancestry. More recently a hundred or more Americans of "Caucasian" ancestry have been ordered to leave their homes and businesses on the west and east coasts after secret hearings by army boards. These arbitrary exercises of executive power through the military have been docilely accepted, even applauded, by most Americans. . . .

Still less has there been any protest against the original presidential order. Yet that order is a complete repudiation of the Anglo-American principle that the lowliest person has rights against the state and is entitled to be judged by his deeds. The order marks the almost unchallenged acceptance of the totalitarian theory that the interest of the state, as interpreted by the executive arm, is the first and last principle of justice. . . .

A further instance of the growth of the totalitarian attitude is the wide demand for, and the insignificant opposition among self styled liberals to, civilian conscription or "total mobilization." . . . It is argued that if soldiers can be drafted to fight, civilians should be drafted to work. But such power cannot be exercised at all efficiently or extensively without enormous practical difficulties and a great strain on morale. Even Nazi Germany did not make the attempt until this year. Civilian conscription along with wage freezing, would reduce labor unions to the level of a labor front. But what is really ominous about the proposal to conscript civilians is the assumption underlying it: that every citizen belongs body and soul to the state which can, if it desires, turn him over to work for another man's profits. Once Americans regarded that as slavery.

Here then is enough evidence of a drift toward totalitarianism. If it be said that conscription and evacuation of populations and the development of arbitrary state power are natural if not inevitable aspects of total war, I will not deny it. But neither is total war a suitable time for complacent optimism among those who cherish freedom. It is not yet lost, but to preserve and strengthen it will require an intelligence and devotion passing anything now evident in the American scene.

RELOCATION OF JAPANESE-AMERICANS

In the spring of 1942, more than 100,000 Japanese-Americans were shipped from the west coast to camps located in various deserted areas throughout the country. About two-thirds of the evacuees were American citizens; none had been charged with any crime. Support for relocation came from several sources: long-standing racial prejudice heightened by the war, a desire for economic gain through the elimination of Japanese competition, and the belief of some politicians that such action would prove popular. Others undoubtedly thought that evacuation was required in order to foil fifth-columnists, although citizens of German and Italian extraction and Japanese in Hawaii were not molested. Responsibility for the removal, however, rested upon the President, Justice Department, and

Army. For many of its victims, evacuation spelled economic hardship, social dislocation, and difficult personal adjustment. Ultimately, in *Korematsu* v. *United States,* the Supreme Court upheld relocation on the grounds that the government was not obliged to respect traditional rights in a national emergency. In a sharp dissent, Justice Robert Jackson said that the decision represented a loaded pistol at the head of every citizen.

29 ★ *Earl Warren,* Testimony on Japanese Evacuation

On February 19, 1942, President Roosevelt issued Executive Order 9066 authorizing the army to designate military areas from which any person might be excluded. A few days later, a Congressional committee under Representative John Tolan heard various west coast public officials describe the threat posed by the Japanese. Earl Warren, then Attorney-General of California, explained why he favored evacuation and revealed the concern felt by normally judicious individuals. [National Defense Migration, Hearings before the Select Committee Investigating National Defense Migration, House of Representatives, Washington, 1942, XXIX, 11010-19.]

For some time I have been of the opinion that the solution of our alien enemy problem with all its ramifications, which include the descendants of aliens, is not only a Federal problem but is a military problem. We believe that all of the decisions in that regard must be made by the military command that is charged with the security of this area. I am convinced that the fifth-column activities of our enemy call for the participation of people who are in fact American citizens, and that if we are to deal realistically with the problem we must realize that we will be obliged in time of stress to deal with subversive elements of our own citizenry.

If that be true, it creates almost an impossible situation for the civil authorities because the civil authorities cannot take protective measures against people of that character. We may suspect their loyalty. We may even have some evidence or, perhaps, substantial evidence of their disloyalty. But until we have the whole pattern of the enemy plan, until we are able to go into court and beyond the exclusion of a reasonable doubt establish the guilt of those elements among our American citizens, there is no way that civil government can cope with the situation.

On the other hand, we believe that in an area, such as in California, which has been designated as a combat zone, when things have happened such as have happened here on the coast, something should be done and done immediately. We believe that any delay in the adoption of the necessary protective measures is to invite disaster. It means that we, too, will have in California a Pearl Harbor incident.

I believe that up to the present and perhaps for a long time to come the greatest danger to continental United States is that from well organized sabotage and fifth-column activity.

Opportunities for Sabotage

California presents, perhaps, the most likely objective in the Nation for such activities. There are many reasons why that is true. First, the size and number of our naval and military establishments in California would make it attractive to our enemies as a field of sabotage. Our geographical position with relation to our enemy and to the war in the Pacific is also a tremendous factor. The number and the diversification of our war industries is extremely vital. The fire hazards due to our climate, our forest areas, and the type of building construction make us very susceptible to fire sabotage. Then the tremendous number of aliens that we have resident here makes it almost an impossible problem from the standpoint of law enforcement.

A wave of organized sabotage in California accompanied by an actual air raid or even by a prolonged black-out could not only be more destructive to life and property but could result in retarding the entire war effort of this Nation far more than the treacherous bombing of Pearl Harbor.

I hesitate to think what the result would be of the destruction of any of our big airplane factories in this State. It will interest you to know that some of our airplane factories in this State are entirely surrounded by Japanese land ownership or occupancy. It is a situation that is fraught with the greatest danger and under no circumstances should it ever be permitted to exist. . . .

To assume that the enemy has not planned fifth column activities for us in a wave of sabotage is simply to live in a fool's paradise. These activities, whether you call them "fifth column activities" or "sabotage" or "war behind the lines upon civilians," or whatever you may call it, are just as much an integral part of Axis warfare as any of their military and naval operations. When I say that I refer to all of the Axis powers with which we are at war.

It has developed into a science and a technique that has been used most effectively against every nation with which the Axis powers are at war. It has been developed to a degree almost beyond the belief of our American citizens. That is one of the reasons it is so difficult for our people to become aroused and appreciate the danger of such activities. Those activities are now being used actively in the war in the Pacific, in every field of operations about which I have read. They have unquestionably, gentlemen, planned such activities for California. For us to believe to the contrary is just not realistic.

Unfortunately, however, many of our people and some of our authorities and, I am afraid, many of our people in other parts of the country are of the opinion that because we have had no sabotage and no fifth column activities in this State since the beginning of the war, that means that none have been planned for us. But I take the view that that is the most ominous sign in our whole situation. It convinces me more than perhaps any other factor that the sabotage that we are to get, the fifth column activities that we are to get, are timed just like Pearl Harbor was timed and just like the invasion of France, and of Denmark, and of Norway, and all of those other countries.

Invisible Deadline for Sabotage

I believe that we are just being lulled into a false sense of security and that the only reason we haven't had disaster in California is because it has been timed for a different date, and that when that time comes if we don't do something about it it is going to mean disaster both to California and to our Nation. Our day of reckoning is bound to come in that regard. When, nobody knows, of course, but we are approaching an invisible deadline.

THE CHAIRMAN: On that point, when that came up in our committee hearings there was not a single case of sabotage reported on the Pacific coast, we heard the heads of the Navy and the Army, and they all tell us that the Pacific coast can be attacked. The sabotage would come coincident with that attack, would it not?

ATTORNEY GENERAL WARREN: Exactly.

THE CHAIRMAN: They would be fools to tip their hands now, wouldn't they?

ATTORNEY GENERAL WARREN: Exactly. If there were sporadic sabotage at this time or if there had been for the last 2 months, the people of California or the Federal authorities would be on the alert to such an extent that they could not possibly have any real fifth column activities when the M-day comes. And I think that that should figure very largely in our conclusions on this subject.

Approaching an invisible deadline as we do, it seems to me that no time can be wasted in making the protective measures that are essential to the security of this State. And when I say "this State" I mean all of the coast, of course. I believe that Oregon and Washington are entitled to the same sort of consideration as the zone of danger as California. Perhaps our danger is intensified by the number of our industries and the number of our aliens, but it is much the same. . . .

Potential Danger from American-Born Japanese

I want to say that the consensus of opinion among the law-enforcement officers of this State is that there is more potential danger among the group of Japanese who are born in this country than from the alien Japanese who were born in Japan. That might seem an anomaly to some people, but the fact is that, in the first place, there are twice as many of them. There are 33,000 aliens and there are 66,000 born in this country.

In the second place, most of the Japanese who were born in Japan are over 55 years of age. There has been practically no migration to this country since 1924. But in some instances the children of those people have been sent to Japan for their education, either in whole or in part, and while they are over there they are indoctrinated with the idea of Japanese imperialism. They receive their religious instruction which ties up their religion with their Emperor, and they come back here imbued with the ideas and the policies of Imperial Japan.

While I do not cast a reflection on every Japanese who is born in this country—of course we will have loyal ones—I do say that the consensus of opinion is that taking the groups by and large there is more potential danger to this State from the group that is born here than from the group that is born in Japan.

MR. ARNOLD: Let me ask you a question at this point.

ATTORNEY GENERAL WARREN: Yes, Congressman.

MR. ARNOLD: Do you have any way of knowing whether any one of this group that you mention is loyal to this country or loyal to Japan?

Many American-born Japanese Educated in Japan

ATTORNEY GENERAL WARREN: Congressman, there is no way that we can establish that fact. We believe that when we are dealing with the Caucasian race we have methods that will test the loyalty of them, and we believe that we can, in dealing with the Germans and the Italians, arrive at some fairly sound conclusions because of our knowledge of the way they live in the community and have lived for many years. But when we deal with the Japanese we are in an entirely different field and we cannot form any opinion that we believe to be sound. Their method of living, their language, make for this difficulty. Many of them who show you a birth certificate stating that they were born in this State, perhaps, or born in Honolulu, can hardly speak the English language because, although they were born here, when they were 4 or 5 years of age they were sent over to Japan to be educated and they stayed over there through their adolescent period at least, and then they came back here thoroughly Japanese. . . .

Vigilantism

There is one thing that concerns us at the present time. As I say, we are very happy over the order of the President yesterday. We believe that is the thing that should be done, but that is only one-half of the problem, as we see it. It is one thing to take these people out of the area and it is another thing to do something with them after they get out. Even from the small areas that they have left up to the present time there are many, many Japanese who are now roaming around the State and roaming around the Western States in a condition that will unquestionably bring about race riots and prejudice and hysteria and excesses of all kind. . . .

My own belief concerning vigilantism is that the people do not engage in vigilante activities so long as they believe that their Government through its agencies is taking care of their most serious problem. But when they get the idea that their problems are not understood, when their Government is not doing for them the things that they believe should be done, they start taking the law into their own hands. . . .

Now, gentlemen, I have some maps which show the character of the Japanese land ownership and possessory interests in California. I will submit them at the time I submit a formal statement on the subject.

These maps show to the law enforcement officers that it is more than just accident, that many of those ownerships are located where they are. We base that assumption not only upon the fact that they are located in certain places, but also on the time when the ownership was acquired.

It seems strange to us that airplane manufacturing plants should be entirely surrounded by Japanese land occupancies. It seems to us that it is more than circumstance that after certain Government air bases were established Japanese undertook farming operations in close proximity to them. You can hardly grow a jackrabbit in some of the places where they presume to be carrying on farming operations close to an Army bombing base.

Many of our vital facilities, and most of our highways are just pocketed by Japanese ownerships that could be of untold danger to us in time of stress.

So we believe, gentlemen, that it would be wise for the military to take every protective measure that it believes is necessary to protect this State and this Nation against the possible activities of these people. . . .

Mr. Sparkman: I do want to add a word to what the chairman said. I am sure you people out here know it, but your congressional delegation in both Houses of Congress has been very much on the alert in discussing and making plans for the defense of this area. A week, 10 days, or 2 weeks ago, this very recommendation was made to the President and, as I read the order, it follows out almost word for word the recommendation that was made by your congressional delegation.

I have noticed suggestions in newspaper stories. I noticed a telegram this morning with reference to the civil rights of these people. What do you have to say about that?

Attorney General Warren: I believe, sir, that in time of war every citizen must give up some of his normal rights.

30 ★ Japanese-Americans Confront Evacuation

Several spokesmen for the Japanese-American community—including Mike Masaoka, Henry Tani, and James Omura—also appeared before the Tolan committee. Their testimony offered insight into some of the dilemmas facing the Nisei and made clear the divisions of opinion that existed. The questions addressed to these witnesses were much sharper than those to Italian-American citizens. [National Defense Migration Hearings, XXIX, 11137, 11144-49, 11229-31.]

MR. SPARKMAN: First, will you give your name to the reporter?

MR. MASAOKA: Just to show you how Americanized we are, I have an English name and Japanese tag-end there. Mike Masaoka, I am the national secretary and field executive of the Japanese American Citizens League. This gentleman is Mr. Dave Tatsuno, president of the San Francisco chapter of the Japanese American Citizens League. And Mr. Henry Tani, the executive secretary of our group. . . .

MR. SPARKMAN: Did you ever attend Japanese schools in this country?

MR. MASAOKA: Personally I did not, but frankly—

MR. SPARKMAN (*interposing*): A great many of your people do?

MR. MASAOKA: Oh, yes. But I did not. . . .

MR. SPARKMAN: What about the membership of your organization? Could you say what percentage of them have received at least a part of their education in Japan?

MR. MASAOKA: Those figures are rather hard to get. We estimate approximately 20 to 30 per cent, which I think is a rather generous estimate.

MR. SPARKMAN: I wonder if you could give us some estimate as to a portion of your membership who have received a part of their education in Japanese schools in this country.

MR. MASAOKA: That would be large; say 85 per cent.

MR. SPARKMAN: That is more or less characteristic, is it not, of the Japanese to have these Japanese schools?

MR. MASAOKA: Yes. It is characteristic, but at the same time I think it is the same as any other immigrant group. I have correspondence here which we will file to show that we have attempted from time to time to get the State of California to include it in their public-school curricula and other evidence of the sort. . . .

I feel that I should make this statement at this time: That before Pearl Harbor many of us had been teaching, or at least attempts had been made to teach, concerning the honor of Japan as a nation. But I think the attack at Pearl Harbor demonstrated to those who were on the fence that there wasn't anything honorable in that, and I think most of us condemned more than Americans condemned the dastardly thing that was done there, and I think the first generation feel that.

MR. SPARKMAN: Do you think you could say with reference to the membership of your organization that there is not a feeling of a definite connection and loyalty to the Emperor of Japan?

MR. MASAOKA: No. I don't think our league subscribes to that. I don't think the great membership of our league subscribe to that. In fact, I am quite sure.

MR. SPARKMAN: Do you think you could truthfully and sincerely say that there is not in your membership a feeling of pride on the accomplishments of the Japanese Empire?

MR. MASAOKA: Well now, there are a lot of things that I think we ought to recognize that are fine about Japan, possibly courtesy, and so on. But I think that the Japan of our parents is certainly not the Japan of today, and I think there that we may have been misguided as to many things there, too. . . .

MR. SPARKMAN: Let me ask you this. Of course, you appreciate that the feeling which you have heard expressed here does exist?

MR. MASAOKA: Yes, I do. I certainly do.

MR. SPARKMAN: You acknowledge that fact. Do I understand that it is your attitude that the Japanese-American citizens do not protest necessarily against an evacuation? They simply want to lodge their claims to consideration?

MR. MASAOKA: Yes.

MR. SPARKMAN: But in the event the evacuation is deemed necessary by those having charge of the defenses, as loyal Americans you are willing to prove your loyalty by cooperating?

MR. MASAOKA: Yes. I think it should be—

MR. SPARKMAN (*interposing*): Even at a sacrifice?

MR. MASAOKA: Oh, yes; definitely. I think that all of us are called upon to make sacrifices. I think that we will be called upon to make greater sacrifices than any others. But I think sincerely, if the military say "Move out," we will be glad to move, because we recognize that even behind evacuation there is not just national security but also a thought as to our own welfare and security because we may be subject to mob violence and otherwise if we are permitted to remain.

MR. SPARKMAN: And it affords you, as a matter of fact, perhaps the best test of your own loyalty?

MR. MASAOKA: Provided that the military or the people charged with the responsibility are cognizant of all the facts. . . .

MR. TANI: . . . With reference to the line of questioning that you are asking Mr. Masaoka, about the influence of the Japanese culture in us. We don't walk around with our heads bowed because we are Japanese, but we can't help being Japanese in features. My mother left Japan over 30 years ago, and the Japan of which she speaks to us of 30 years ago is not the Japan of today. I feel it is different from that of my mother's day. And so in the culture that she instilled in us, and by "culture" I mean courtesy, loyalty to the State and country in which we are, obedience to parents, those are cultures of Japan with which most of us have been brought up. And I don't think those things are things of which we should be ashamed, those things which we should ignore.

As for influences upon us today I, as an individual, or as a leader of a group, have never been approached officially, unofficially, directly, or indirectly in any respect in all my years.

MR. OMURA: . . . I am strongly opposed to mass evacuation of American-born Japanese. It is my honest belief that such an action would not solve the question of Nisei loyalty. If any such action is taken I believe that we would be only procrastinating on the question of loyalty, that we are afraid to deal with it, and that at this, our first opportunity, we are trying to strip the Nisei of their opportunity to prove their loyalty.

I do not believe there has ever been, or ever could be again, a situation of this kind where the Nisei can prove their loyalty.

I suppose you understand that I am in some measure opposed to what some of the other representatives of the Japanese community have said here before this committee. . . .

It is doubtlessly rather difficult for Caucasian Americans to properly comprehend and believe in what we say. Our citizenship has even been attacked as an evil cloak under which we expect immunity for the nefarious purpose of conspiring to destroy the American way of life. To us—who have been born, raised, and educated in American institutions and in our system of public schools, knowing and owing no other allegiance than to the United States—such a thought is manifestly unfair and ambiguous.

I would like to ask the committee: Has the Gestapo come to America? Have we not risen in righteous anger at Hitler's mistreatments of the Jews? Then, is it not incongruous that citizen Americans of

Japanese descent should be similarly mistreated and persecuted? I speak from a humanitarian standpoint and from a realistic and not a theoretical point of view. This view, I believe, does not endanger the national security of this country nor jeopardize our war efforts. . . .

We cannot understand why General DeWitt can make exceptions for families of German and Italian soldiers in the armed forces of the United States while ignoring the civil rights of the Nisei Americans. Are we to be condemned merely on the basis of our racial origin? Is citizenship such a light and transient thing that that which is our inalienable right in normal times can be torn from us in times of war?

THE NEGRO AND THE WAR

The war improved the Negro's social and economic position, but it also inflamed racial tension. On June 25, 1941, President Roosevelt, faced with a threatened Negro march on Washington, issued Executive Order 8802, which prohibited discrimination in defense contracts and created a Fair Employment Practices Committee. By the end of 1944, nearly 2 million Negroes were employed in munitions and defense plants; in addition, the traditional bars to their employment as skilled workers were crumbling. At the same time, civil rights organizations adopted a militant stance, asserted that racial discrimination was inconsistent with the Four Freedoms, and called for a "Double Victory" at home and abroad. Many Southerners responded to the drive for Negro rights with a strident determination to preserve Jim Crow. In the north, large-scale migrations to industrial centers and increased proximity of Negroes and whites in employment led to racial conflict that sometimes erupted into violence. Nevertheless, the war brought the concept of white supremacy into disrepute and created conditions under which the civil rights movement could make important gains.

31 ★ *J. Saunders Redding, "A Negro Looks at This War"*

Although some Negroes who recalled the empty rhetoric accompanying World War I expressed reservations about their stake in an American victory after 1941, apprehension that Negroes would not support the war proved ill-founded. Adam Clayton Powell, Jr., for example, claimed that Southern racists were no better than Nazis, but concluded that the conflict was not just a "white man's war." In the following essay, the well-known author J. Saunders Redding discussed

the considerations that led him to support the war. [American Mercury,
LV (November 1942), 585-92. Reprinted by permission of *American
Mercury*, Box 1306, Torrance, California.]

I was listening sleeplessly to an all-night program of music interspersed with war news, bad news. The bad news of the war had not seemed bad news to me. Indeed, on this night, it was again giving me a kind of grim, perverted satisfaction. Some non-white men were killing some white men and it might be that the non-whites would win. This gratified me in a way difficult to explain. Perhaps, in a world conquered and ruled by yellow men, there would be no onus attached to being black and I, a Negro. . . . Then a peculiar thing happened. Something seemed to burst and I knew suddenly that I believed in this war we Americans are fighting. I think I said aloud, and with a kind of wonder: "I, a Negro, believe in this war we Americans are fighting." The thought or revelation gave rise to an emotion—keen, purging, astringent.

The thought and the conviction amazed me, for I had thought that I could never believe in war again, or that any war in which I might believe would be truly a race war; and then, naturally, I would believe as I had been taught by innumerable circumstances to believe. I would believe in the side of the darker peoples. But I could envision no such war even in the remote future, for I had been trained in the principles called Christian. I had been trained to believe in the brotherhood of man and that we were approaching that glorious state—slowly, but before complete catastrophe could overtake us.

War had no heroic traditions for me. Wars were white folks'. All wars in historical memory. The last war, and the Spanish-American War before that, and the Civil War. I had been brought up in a way that admitted of no heroics. I think my parents were right. Life for them was a fierce, bitter, soul-searing war of spiritual and economic attrition; they fought it without heroics, but with stubborn heroism. Their heroism was screwed up to a pitch of idealism so intense that it found a safety valve in cynicism about the heroics of white folks' war. This cynicism went back at least as far as my paternal grandmother, whose fierce eyes used to lash the faces of her five grandchildren as she said, "An' he done som'pin big an' brave away down dere to Chickymorgy an' dey made a iron image of him 'cause he got his head blowed off an' his stomick blowed out fightin' to keep his slaves." I cannot convey the scorn and the cynicism she put into her picture of that hero-son of her slave-master, but I have never forgotten.

I was nearly ten when we entered the last war in 1917. The European fighting, and the sinking of the *Lusitania,* had seemed as remote, as distantly meaningless to us, as the Battle of Hastings. Then we went in and suddenly the city was flag-draped, slogan-plastered, and as riotously gay as on circus half-holidays. I remember one fine Sunday we came upon an immense new billboard with a new slogan: GIVE! TO MAKE THE WORLD SAFE FOR DEMOCRACY. My brother, who was the oldest of us, asked what making the world safe for democracy meant. My father frowned, but before he could answer, my mother broke in.

"It's just something to say, like . . ."—and then she was stuck until she hit upon one of the family's old jokes—"like 'Let's make a million dollars.'" We all laughed, but the bitter core of her meaning lay revealed, even for the youngest of us, like the stone in a halved peach. . . .

I remember that first, false, mad Armistice. Everyone seemed crazy drunk and everywhere there was a spontaneous and unabashed breakdown of lines. Banker and butcher, coal-heaver and clerk, black and white, men and women went worming and screaming joyously through the streets. I also remember the real Armistice, and that there was a block party which Negroes could not attend, and that the police would not give them a permit to hold one of their own in the narrow, factory-flanked streets where most of them lived. When the lynchings and the riots started again—in East St. Louis, Chicago, Chester, even in Washington—we knew that, so far as the Negro was concerned, the war had been a failure, and "making the world safe for democracy" a good phrase bandied about by weak or blind or unprincipled men.

And so, since I have reached maturity and thought a man's thoughts and had a man's—a Negro man's—experiences, I have thought that I could never believe in war again. Yet I believe in this one.

There are many things about this war that I do not like, just as there are many things about "practical" Christianity that I do not like. But I believe in Christianity, and if I accept the shoddy and unfulfilling in the conduct of this war, I do it as voluntarily and as purposefully as I accept the trash in the workings of "practical" Christianity. I do not like the odor of political pandering that arises from some groups. I do not like these "race incidents" in the camps. I do not like the world's not knowing officially that there were Negro soldiers on Bataan with General Wainwright. I do not like the constant references to the Japs as "yellow bastards," "yellow bellies," and "yellow monkeys," as if color had something to do with treachery, as if color were the issue and the thing we are fighting rather than oppression, slavery, and a way of life hateful and nauseating. These and other things I do not like, yet I believe in the war.

The issue is plain. The issue, simply, is freedom. Freedom is a precious thing. Proof of its preciousness is that so many men wait patiently for its fulfillment, accept defilement and insult in the hope of it, die in the attainment of it. It used to seem shamefully silly to me to hear Negroes talk about freedom. But now I know that we Negroes here in America know a lot about freedom and love it more than a great many people who have long had it. . . .

We go through a stage of blind, willful delusion. Later, we come to see that in the logic of a system based on freedom and the dignity of man we have a chance. We see that now and again there are advances. And this new seeing kindles the hope that Americans are really not proud of their silly prejudices, their thick-skinned discriminations, their expensive segregations. And now, I think, we know that whatever the mad logic of the New Order, there is no hope for us under it. The ethnic theories of the Hitler "master folk" admit of no chance of freedom, but rather glory in its expungement.

This is a war to keep men free. The struggle to broaden and lengthen the road of freedom—our own private and important war to enlarge freedom here in America—will come later. That this private, intra-American war will be carried on and won is the only real reason we Negroes have to fight. We must keep the road open. Did we not believe in a victory in that intra-American war, we could not believe in nor stomach the compulsion of this. If we could not believe in the realization of democratic freedom for ourselves, certainly no one could ask us to die for the preservation of that ideal for others. But to broaden and lengthen the road of freedom is different from preserving it. And our first duty is to keep the road of freedom open. It must be done continuously. It is the duty of the whole people to do this. Our next duty (and this, too, is the whole people's) is to broaden that road so that more people can travel it without snarling traffic. To die in these duties is to die for something. . . .

I believe in this war, finally, because I believe in the ultimate vindication of the wisdom of the brotherhood of man. This is not foggy idealism. I think that the growing manifestations of the interdependence of all men is an argument for the wisdom of brotherhood. I think that the shrunk compass of the world is an argument. I think that the talk of united nations and of planned interdependence is an argument.

More immediately, I believe in this war because I believe in America. I believe in what America professes to stand for. Nor is this, I think, whistling in the dark. There are a great many things wrong here. There are only a few men of good will. I do not lose sight of that. I know the inequalities, the outraged hopes and faith, the inbred hate; and I know that there are people who wish merely to lay these by in the closet of the national mind until the crisis is over. But it would be equally foolish for me to lose sight of the advances that are made, the barriers that are leveled, the privileges that grow. Foolish, too, to remain blind to the distinction that exists between simple race prejudice, already growing moribund under the impact of this war, and theories of racial superiority as a basic tenet of a societal system—theories that at bottom are the avowed justification for suppression, defilement and murder.

I will take this that I have here. I will take the democratic theory. The bit of road of freedom that stretches through America is worth fighting to preserve. The very fact that I, a Negro in America, can fight against the evils in America is worth fighting for. This open fighting against the wrongs one hates is the mark and the hope of democratic freedom. I do not underestimate the struggle. I know the learning that must take place, the evils that must be broken, the depths that must be climbed. But I am free to help in doing these things. I count. I am free (though only a little as yet) to pound blows at the huge body of my American world until, like a chastened mother, she gives me nurture with the rest.

32 ★ *Thurgood Marshall,* "The Gestapo in Detroit"

In June, 1943, Detroit was the scene of a race riot which lasted 36 hours and took 34 lives. The riot had its roots in social instability resulting from a massive influx of war workers. In a report to city officials, the police commissioner admitted that his men "made many mistakes," but insisted that on the whole they "demonstrated rare courage, efficiency, and . . . good judgment." Thurgood Marshall, chief counsel for the NAACP, presented a different view of the riot, one held by a great many Negroes. [The Crisis, L (August 1943), 232-33, 246-47. Reprinted by permission.]

Riots are usually the result of many underlying causes, yet no single factor is more important than the attitude and efficiency of the police. When disorder starts, it is either stopped quickly or permitted to spread into serious proportions, depending upon the actions of the local police.

Much of the blood spilled in the Detroit riot is on the hands of the Detroit police department. In the past the Detroit police have been guilty of both inefficiency and an attitude of prejudice against Negroes. Of course, there are several individual exceptions. . . .

In the June riot of this year, the police ran true to form. The trouble reached riot proportions because the police once again enforced the law with an unequal hand. They used "persuasion" rather than firm action with white rioters, while against Negroes they used the ultimate in force: night sticks, revolvers, riot guns, sub-machine guns, and deer guns. As a result, 25 of the 34 persons killed were Negroes. Of the latter, 17 were killed by police.

The excuse of the police department for the disproportionate number of Negroes killed is that the majority of them were shot while committing felonies: namely, the looting of stores on Hastings street. On the other hand, the crimes of arson and felonious assaults are also felonies. It is true that some Negroes were looting stores and were shot while committing these crimes. It is equally true that white persons were turning over and burning automobiles on Woodward avenue. This is arson. Others were beating Negroes with iron pipes, clubs, and rocks. This is felonious assault. Several Negroes were stabbed. This is assault with intent to murder.

All these crimes are matters of record. Many were committed in the presence of police officers, several on the pavement around the City Hall. Yet the record remains: Negroes killed by police—17; white persons killed by police—none. The entire record, both of the riot killings and of previous disturbances, reads like the story of the Nazi Gestapo. . . .

Belle Isle is a municipal recreation park where thousands of white and Negro war workers and their families go on Sundays for their outings. There had been isolated instances of racial friction in the past. On Sunday night, June 20, there was trouble between a group of white and Negro people. The disturbance was under control by midnight. During the time of the disturbance and after it was under control, the police searched the automobiles of all Negroes and searched the Negroes as well. They did not search the white people. One Negro who was to be inducted into the army the following week was arrested because another person in the car had a small pen knife. This youth was later sentenced to 90 days in jail before his family could locate him. Many Negroes were arrested during this period and rushed to local police stations. At the very beginning the police demonstrated that they would continue to handle racial disorders by searching, beating and arresting Negroes while using mere persuasion on white people.

A short time after midnight disorder broke out in a white neighborhood near the Roxy theatre on Woodward avenue. The Roxy is an all night theatre attended by white and Negro patrons. Several Negroes were beaten and others were forced to remain in the theatre for lack of police protection. The rumor spread among the white people that a Negro had raped a white woman on Belle Island and that the Negroes were rioting.

At about the same time a rumor spread around Hastings and Adams streets in the Negro area that white sailors had thrown a Negro woman and her baby into the lake at Belle Isle and that the police were beating Negroes. This rumor was also repeated by an unidentified Negro at one of the night spots. Some Negroes began to attack white persons in the area. The police immediately began to use their sticks and revolvers against them. The Negroes began to break out the windows of stores of white merchants on Hastings street.

The interesting thing is that when the windows in the stores on Hastings street were first broken, there was no looting. An officer of the Merchants' Association walked the length of Hastings street, starting 7 o'clock Monday morning and noticed that none of the stores with broken windows had been looted. It is thus clear that the original breaking of windows was not for the purpose of looting.

Throughout Monday the police, instead of placing men in front of the stores to protect them from looting, contented themselves with driving up and down Hastings street from time to time stopping in front of the stores. The usual procedure was to jump out of the squad cars with drawn revolvers and riot guns to shoot whoever might be in the store. The policemen would then tell the Negro bystanders to "run and not look back." On several occasions, persons running were shot in the back. In other instances, bystanders were clubbed by police. To the police, all Negroes on Hastings street were "looters." This included war workers returning from work. There is no question that many Negroes were guilty of looting, just as there is always looting during earthquakes or as there was when English towns were bombed by the Germans.

Woodward avenue is one of the main thoroughfares of the city of Detroit. Small groups of white people began to rove up and down Woodward beating Negroes, stoning cars containing Negroes, stopping street cars and yanking Negroes from them, and stabbing and shooting Negroes. In no case did the police do more than try to "reason" with these mobs, many of which were, at this stage, quite small. The police did not draw their revolvers or riot guns, and never used any force to disperse these mobs. As a result of this, the mobs got larger and bolder and even attacked Negroes on the pavement of the City Hall in demonstration not only of their contempt for Negroes, but of their contempt for law and order as represented by the municipal government.

During this time, Mayor Jeffries was in his office in the City Hall with the door locked and the window shade drawn. The use of night sticks or the drawing of revolvers would have dispersed these white groups and saved the lives of many Negroes. It would not have been necessary to shoot, but it would have been sufficient to threaten to shoot into the white mobs. The use of a fire hose would have dispersed many of the groups. None of these things was done and the disorder took on the proportions of a major riot. The responsibility rests with the Detroit police. . . .

33 ★ A Southern View of the Negro Question

Frank Boykin had represented Mobile, Alabama, in Congress since 1935. When his constituents complained about the employment of Negroes in federal agencies, Boykin expressed his indignation at government policy to the President's personal secretary, Edwin M. Watson. On March 6, 1943 Boykin wrote to Watson: "It will be very difficult to break up the solid South, and there is only one thing that will really do it, and that is this race question." [Franklin D. Roosevelt Papers, Official File 93.]

. . . I know you understand our problem and if we were just left alone with this question we could handle it without any trouble. . . .

This just won't do in our country. There is no one who can make our people stand for it and we need the President's help in this matter. Our people in Mobile and the entire South are very staunch "Rock of Gibraltar" democrats. Do not forget that when the whole country turned against the Democratic Party and elected Hoover, that Alabama stayed right in the column and we voted solid for Al Smith. It is difficult for me to express the way our people feel about this matter. They are really more upset about this than they are about the war and I really believe our people would rather be dead than have to put up with the negro men giving our white women orders. As a matter of fact, I know they had. . . .

All of my family have always been in all of our wars and we have always been Democrats and will be until we die. We do not believe that our great President will subject us to this treatment that we have never had to put up with in our lives and since we have been a Nation. We depend on him and we know he will not fail us. . . . In coming back from Jacksonville a few weeks ago, I heard the same thing there, the same thing in Alabama, Mississippi and Georgia. It seems to be worse in Georgia than any other place, and as I have said before, not only is Alabama, but the whole South is upset on this race question.

CONSCIENTIOUS OBJECTORS

The treatment of conscientious objectors depended very largely upon the nature of their opposition to the war. The Selective Service Act exempted only those who dissented "by reason of religious training and belief." Although many kinds of people claimed conscientious objection, most who did so were members of the historic peace churches (Mennonites, Brethren, Quakers), Jehovah's Witnesses, or philosophical pacifists. The majority of conscientious objectors served as noncombatants in the armed forces; more than 25,000 pursued this course and suffered no penalty. Those unwilling to be inducted could work in Civilian Public Service camps, jointly administered by the peace churches and the Selective Service system. Some 12,000 men served in this way, fighting forest fires, combatting hookworm in depressed rural areas, working in mental hospitals, and volunteering as subjects for medical experiments. They received no pay, no compensation in case of injury, and their dependents received no government assistance. Finally, those who could not accept compulsory work were imprisoned; 5500 men went to jail, three-fourths of them Jehovah's Witnesses. Nearly three times as many conscientious objectors were imprisoned, in proportion to those conscripted, as in World War I. The government's primary concern was always with manpower, morale, and public opinion. Within these limits, it was ready to respect the conscience of those whose opinions derived from religious belief, who could perform nonmilitary compulsory labor and risk impoverishment.

34 ★ *A. J. Muste,* "Reflections on the Problems of COs in Prison"

Civilian Public Service provided a way for some conscientious objectors to perform important tasks, but those who refused to register for the draft or who were denied classification as conscientious objectors were imprisoned. The following article by A. J. Muste, a noted pacifist, represented the views of the Fellowship of Reconciliation. It assessed some of the implications of the conflict between individual conscience and submission to state authority. [Fellowship, X (January 1944), 10, 14. Copyright by the Fellowship of Reconciliation. Reprinted by permission.]

Three attitudes are found among COs who, either because they were "absolutists" or because they were refused IV-E classification and would not submit to induction into the armed forces, have been sentenced to Federal prisons.

I

So far, the great majority have submitted to prison regulations and have been "cooperative" in their attitude toward prison officials. There have been instances where they were called upon to do work which seemed to them to contribute directly to the war effort. They have protested quietly in such ways as were available in prison, and so far as we know always have been put quite promptly on other work. COs in this group also have worked for correction of other conditions in prison, with satisfaction to themselves and often to the prison officials. They have found opportunities to help fellow prisoners in various ways and to exemplify their conception of the spirit and the methods of brotherhood and reconciliation. Authorities have spoken enthusiastically of the influence exerted by such men over other prisoners, and similar testimony has come from non-CO prisoners themselves.

II

A small but apparently growing number of COs feel that they must take an "absolutist" position against the whole Federal prison regime. They are in prison because of their conscience-impelled opposition to war and conscription; how, they ask, can they be expected to change to an attitude of cooperation with these when the conscription regime perpetrates the further evil of throwing them into prison? The only consistent course for them, they feel, is to refuse cooperation and take the consequences.

There is the feeling also that the Federal prison regime—any modern prison regime—is in itself a major evil, corrupt and corrupting, an embodiment of the authoritarian attitude as truly as war itself or conscription. In some of the non-cooperating COs, this feeling exists alongside the former; in others it is perhaps the dominant one.

III

A few COs whose general attitude has been a cooperative, "non-absolutist" one, have been led to engage in work or hunger strikes over specific issues. The refusal of the authorities in the Danbury and Lewisburg prisons to permit Negroes and whites to sit at an interracial table in the dining-room has been such an issue, as have the censorship of prison mail and the refusal to allow prisoners books and writing materials.

Points for Consideration

The following points deserve the careful consideration of all pacifists, and in particular those COs in prison who feel called upon to follow a course of protest and non-cooperation.

It can be argued that the whole modern system of statism and regimentation is a *growing* evil, not a regime that is being reformed and improved or that is on the way out. Many feel, therefore, that total opposition must be set against it.

However, it must be remembered that the prison system antedates modern totalitarianism. It is not accurate to call it simply and completely a part of conscription. All who are competent to judge seem to agree that the last century has seen progress in prison reform, with notable improvements in the Federal prison system within the past decade.

Great as are the abuses that still prevail, it thus may well be valid for a pacifist to say: "My fight is against war and conscription. I will carry that fight on so far as I am left in freedom, no matter what the consequences. Once the State shows its hand and reveals that it has no place for the free man except prison, I have made my point. I will submit to the ordinary prison regime, trying to improve it in such ways as are open to me, using my opportunities to interpret pacifism to my fellow inmates, and working to regain my freedom and that of other pacifists in order to resume our work against war and conscription."

The fact that a considerable number of the most deeply spiritual and courageous COs have taken this attitude certainly should give pause to those who incline to an opposite course. Gandhi's life is devoted to Satyagraha, a witness for the way of truth and non-violence, and to the achievement of independence for India by non-violent means. As a result of his work and life, he has been imprisoned often. During imprisonment he has engaged in fasts—though not "unto death"—but for the most part, he seems to have been a submissive prisoner. This in spite of the fact that it could be argued that British jails in India are an integral part of British domination—i.e., of the system against which Gandhi is contending—and the well-known fact that there are grave abuses in the prison system in India.

By and large, virtually all prophets and revolutionists in history, secular and religious, have pursued the same policy in prison as has Gandhi. They are concerned first of all about some social objective—in Gandhi's case, independence for India and abolition of untouchability. What they want is to work in freedom for that objective. When they are deprived of that freedom, they want to get out, and their comrades want them to get out, to continue that work. There is a danger that in submitting to ordinary prison regulations they are compromising with evil, and certainly they must not become insensitive to that danger; but adopting an over-all policy of non-submission also has its dangers.

The pacifist movement today has a tremendous job on its hand, including getting COs out of jail, stopping the war, etc. We ought to consider pretty carefully how that may be done most effectively, and recognize that such consideration involves no moral dereliction. It is legitimate that those who propose to undertake an unconventional course should consider carefully whether they may be diverting a movement from its main course, and, in effect, coercing it into devoting undue attention to a "concern" of a small minority. . . .

"All Possible Support"

While this memo has placed much stress upon considerations which I believe actual or prospective "non-cooperators" should have in mind, we must recognize also that such men as these in the past often have proven to be true pioneers, and that men of other dispositions who follow other paths also are subject to peculiar temptations against which they need to guard.

Certainly those who follow a policy of "cooperation" with the persons involved in a situation need to be on guard lest in effect this means submission to a tolerance of or cooperation with the evil in the situation. A policy of "cooperation" is valid only if it grows out of a thorough-going disassociation from that evil. I am convinced also that it is dangerous to regard one technique among several as necessarily the highest expression of the spirit of love, "the Way of the Cross." That spirit may be equally present in men who follow diverse courses, as COs in prison have themselves freely recognized.

The "non-cooperators" already have brought certain serious abuses to public attention—even to the attention of prison officials, who were not previously aware of the existence of these abuses. Notable improvements are being made with regard to censorship of mail and admission of books and other reading matter in Federal prisons. As the National Council stated at its annual meeting, we have confidence in the honesty and integrity of our COs in prison. We are clear that we must continue to follow the policy that we feel has stood the test of experience, that is, of giving all possible support to individuals and groups in acting according to conscience.

35 ★ *The Christian Century,* "The Christian and the War"

> *Because Civilian Public Service provided a legal status for those refusing to bear arms, it raised problems for the sincere objector. Some of the ways in which modern warfare and government policy tended to undermine the pacifist position were pointed out by a prominent nonpacifist Protestant journal. [The Christian Century, LIX (January 28, 1942), 102-4. Reprinted by permission.]*

We are all in the war—Christians and non-Christians, pacifists and non-pacifists. And we are all fighting—Christians and non-Christians, pacifists and non-pacifists. We may deplore the fact, we may resent the necessity, we may cry out in anguish of soul against it, but we cannot escape it. The Christian pacifist is in the fight with all the rest of us. He has no alternative. He accepts the war as his war and fights for victory. There are no exceptions. The Quakers fight, the Mennonites and Brethren fight, the members of the Fellowship of Reconciliation fight, the pacifist preachers fight—despite their vows never to support war again. These all fight by virtue of their implication in the indivisible solidarity of their national community whose total resources, including the pacifist himself and his job and all his civilian duties and activities, are integrated in one vast military machine. The pacifist cannot get out of this fighting machine, try as he may. But—save for a small minority of pacifists whose course we shall consider presently—he does not even try to escape it. He accepts the war as a necessity, and fights to win it.

But the pacifist goes farther than passive acceptance of the necessity. He takes an attitude of positive participation, though he defines this attitude negatively. He declares that he will not obstruct the fighting activities of his country. This is the standard formula for the pacifist position in wartime. It is stated by the Fellowship of Reconciliation thus: "We will not oppose, obstruct or interfere with officials, soldiers or civilians in the performance of what they regard as their patriotic duty." This is not merely a negative position; it has its positive side. It means that the pacifist will *help* his country to win by not obstructing its war effort. It is a belligerent position, not a neutral one. It is taken because the pacifist positively prefers victory for his own country to victory for the enemy country. He cannot shake himself free of this preference without perverting his natural manhood.

In peacetime, when the pacific processes of history are open, the pacifist may advocate policies which involve large sacrifices by his own nation in the interest of justice. He may even advocate the surrender by his nation of certain of its powers, privileges or possessions in order to remove the festering injustices which breed war. He may contend that "patriotism is not enough"; that above the nation stands humanity, and that national interest must be qualified by the right of all peoples to have equitable access to the goods of nature and science. In doing this he will be standing on indisputably Christian ground. The pacifist will do well, however, to remember that these views are not peculiar to his school of thought, but common to all Christians, non-pacifists no less than pacifists.

But in war this principle of "humanity first" is thrown to the winds. The pacifist can find no opening to act upon it. In war, the nation needs and clutches to itself every advantage of wealth, privilege, power that it possesses or can seize. To talk of surrendering any of these advantages in wartime is equivalent to conniving at the nation's defeat. The pacifist, involved in actual war, confronts, like all his fellow citizens, one question, and only one, a sharp and narrow question: Do I prefer victory or defeat for my country? He prefers victory, and says so, distinctly, when he declares that he will not obstruct his country's effort to win the victory. . . .

There is nothing which pacifists believe and nothing they do or stand ready to do which multitudes of non-pacifists do not believe and do—except at one point, and that is the actual bearing of arms. But the practical incidence of the pacifist's refusal to bear arms falls upon only a small minority of pacifists—it falls only upon those men who come within the scope of the draft as eligible for the fighting services. They alone confront the necessity, or have the privilege, of making a decision which is in any degree relevant to the essential pacifist belief.

This means that the burden of pacifism, the whole burden, rests upon the young pacifist draftee. How successful is he in escaping the common necessity? He refuses to bear arms. In earlier wars, this seemed a sufficient testimony to his pacifist belief. Wars were fought by volunteers. He simply did not volunteer. Total war was not then known as "total," though in reality it was total. The separation between civilian life and army life seemed obvious, and the conscience of the non-volunteering objector to war rested unperturbed as he went on raising food on his farm which went to the army, or forging arms or making clothes in the factory for soldiers, or pursuing his vocation, whatever it might be, in a manner that kept up the nation's morale, but meanwhile refraining from any obstructive activity.

Now, however, we know that war is total. The distinction between civilian life and soldier life no longer exists. It has been wiped out by the fact, as stated by General Hershey, director of the national selective service, that the civilian labor of from fourteen to twenty-five workers is required to keep one fighting man at the front. Volunteering has given place to conscription. All within certain age limits must register and accept assignment somewhere in the ranks, whether with those who bear arms or with those who produce arms, equipment, food and other things necessary for the prosecution of the war.

This explicit involvement of the whole population in the war has presented the youthful pacifist with a problem of which his pacifist grandfather was not conscious. The issue which he faces does not now lie within his power to decide in the absolutist manner in which the grandfather imagined that he could decide it. The issue has now been shifted from the simple bearing of arms to the right of the state to compel him to accept *any* form of participation in the war. He challenges the right of the state to do this.

In the other World War the whole issue turned upon the pacifist's unwillingness to recognize this right. He refused to register, and went to prison for the duration of the war. But in this war, both here and in

Great Britain, a more merciful law has been enacted, a law which recognizes the right of the citizen to be a conscientious objector and provides an alternative form of service, called "work of national importance," to which the government, convinced of his sincerity, may assign him. . . .

The government, operating explicitly on a "total war" basis, has thus with a mixture of mercy and shrewdness arranged the situation so as to becloud and largely nullify the witness "against war" which the conscientious objector desires to make by undergoing suffering and social stigma such as was frequently endured before conscription was introduced in World War I. Even in that war, the objector who refused to register, or who refused "non-combatant" service, was imprisoned for the duration of the war and endured extreme persecution at the hands of the authorities and their fellow prisoners. But now, the religious conscientious objector is recognized by law and treated by the administrators of the law, save in rare cases, with humane consideration.

While this newly achieved legal status has deprived the pacifist witness of much of the carrying power and significance with which poignant sacrifice and suffering formerly invested it, the reality of the pacifist's witness has been greatly narrowed by the technical refinements through which he is compelled by total war to bear it. His action no longer possesses that gross realism which it seemed to have when the assumption prevailed that warfare was one thing and civilian life another, and that by refusing to bear arms one could avoid participation in war. . . .

Total war has thus pushed the pacifist draftee into a narrow corner, and made available so many technical options that his protest or witness has taken on the character of arbitrariness and artificiality. It has also made the effects of conscientious objection so easy to bear (compared to the lot of the soldier) that his witness has been rendered ambiguous. At the same time, total war has revealed the impossibility of escape from the solidarity of the national community whose total population is regimented in one vast fighting army.

36 ★ *Franklin D. Roosevelt,* Conscientious Objectors and the State

In April, 1943, Norman Thomas urged the President to endorse "detached service" on farms and in hospitals for objectors. Thomas hoped that they could be paid at the same rate as soldiers; he thought, however, that any wages taken by the government should be placed in a nonmilitary fund. On May 20, 1943, Roosevelt replied, setting

forth the official view of the obligations of conscientious objectors.
[Franklin D. Roosevelt Papers, Official File 111.]

Since conscientious objectors, classified as IV-E, have been selected
to serve their country under the same law as men are selected for service
in the armed forces, their status is parallel and they should expect no
more freedom and choice of action. Their time and energy belongs to
the Government and their services should be utilized in performing such
projects as will best aid the Government in this emergency, keeping in
mind the limitations imposed by the law. The needs of the Government
are paramount to the desires of the individual. When the house is on
fire the doctor and clergyman help the firemen to rescue the victims.
After they are rescued, the doctor ministers to their physical needs and
the clergyman to their spiritual needs and the firemen put out the fire.
The agency responsible must decide whether the interest of the Government will be served best by group or individual assignment under the
circumstances. . . .

Assignees performing work of national importance are receiving
compensation in the form of food, clothing, shelter, medical care, al-
lowances and other services. The fact that these things are supplied by
other agencies than Selective Service does not alter the situation as they
are provided for by law. Whether the amount they receive is commen-
surate with that of a soldier is a matter of opinion when the risks of
service are considered. The law does not say that they should be paid
the same wage as soldiers but only that they should not be paid more.

5 The Social Impact of War

FAMILIES ON THE MOVE

During World War II, more than 15.3 million civilians moved across county lines. Although redistribution of the population occurred in an uneven fashion, the general flow of migration was from the country to the city and from east to west. Two million people moved to a half-dozen major cities, including Los Angeles, San Francisco, and Detroit; a great many smaller communities also were transformed into boom towns. Inevitably, migration placed strains upon families that were required to adjust to a strange environment while living in badly crowded quarters. The lack of adequate schools, playgrounds, and health facilities presented additional difficulties. Migration also disturbed patterns of social behavior in established communities. Newcomers, often regarding themselves as transients, were less subject to informal community restraints and less ready to assume social obligations than were natives. Then too, the segregated housing of war workers prevented much personal association with older residents. For some families, migration undoubtedly spelled excitement, diversity, and economic improvement; for others, it brought severe problems of personal and social adjustment.

37 ★ *John Dos Passos, "Gold Rush Down South"*

Mobile, Alabama was one of the cities poorly equipped to deal with the immense problems that came with the migration of war workers. John Dos Passos, who visited Mobile in March, 1943, described the nature of the migrants and their impact upon the city. [State of the Nation (Boston: Houghton Mifflin Company, 1944), pp. 92-94, 99. Reprinted by permission of the author.]

The mouldering old Gulf seaport with its ancient dusty elegance of tall shuttered windows under mansard roofs and iron lace overgrown with vines, and scaling colonnades shaded by great trees, looks trampled and battered like a city that's been taken by storm. Sidewalks are crowded. Gutters are stacked with litter that drifts back and forth in the brisk spring wind. Garbage cans are overflowing. Frame houses on treeshaded streets bulge with men in shirtsleeves who spill out onto the porches and trampled grassplots and stand in knots at the streetcorners. There's still talk of lodginghouses where they rent 'hot beds.' (Men work in three shifts. Why shouldn't they sleep in three shifts?) Cues wait outside of movies and lunchrooms. The trailer army has filled all the open lots with its regular ranks. In cluttered backyards people camp out in tents and chickenhouses and shelters tacked together out of packingcases.

In the outskirts in every direction you find acres and acres raw with new building, open fields skinned to the bare clay, elevations gashed with muddy roads and gnawed out by the powershovels and the bulldozers. There long lines of small houses, some decently planned on the 'American standard' model and some mere boxes with a square brick chimney on the center, miles of dormitories, great squares of temporary structures are knocked together from day to day by a mob of construction workers in a smell of paint and freshsawed pine lumber and tobacco juice and sweat. Along the river for miles has risen a confusion of new yards from which men, women, and boys ebb and flow three times a day. Here and there are whole city blocks piled with wreckage and junk as if ancient cranky warehouses and superannuated stores had caved in out of their own rottenness under the impact of the violence of the new effort. Over it all the Gulf mist, heavy with smoke of soft coal, hangs in streaks, and glittering the training planes endlessly circle above the airfields.

. . . To be doing something towards winning the war, to be making some money, to learn a trade, men and women have been pouring into the city for more than a year now; tenants from dusty shacks set on stilts above the bare eroded earth in the midst of the cotton and the scraggly corn, small farmers and trappers from halfcultivated patches in the piney woods, millhands from the industrial towns in the northern part of the state, garage men, fillingstation attendants, storekeepers, drugclerks from crossroads settlements, longshore fishermen and oystermen, negroes off plantations who've never seen any town but the county seat on Saturday afternoon, white families who've lived all their lives off tobacco and 'white meat' and cornpone in cranky cabins forgotten in the hills.

For them everything's new and wonderful. They can make more spot cash in a month than they saw before in half a year. They can buy radios, they can go to the pictures, they can go to beerparlors, bowl, shoot craps, bet on the ponies. Everywhere they rub elbows with foreigners from every state in the Union. Housekeeping in a trailer with electric light and running water is a dazzling luxury to a woman who's lived all her life in a cabin with half-inch chinks between the splintered boards of the floor. There are street cars and busses to take you anywhere you want to go. At night the streets are bright with electric light. Girls can go to beautyparlors, get their nails manicured, buy readymade dresses. In the backwoods a girl who's reached puberty feels she's a woman. She's never worried much about restraining her feelings when she had any. Is it any wonder that they can't stay home at dusk when the streets fill up with hungry boys in uniforms? . . .

And all the while, by every bus and train the new people, white and black, pour into the city. As fast as a new block of housing is finished, it's jampacked. As soon as a new bus is put into service, it's weighed down with passengers. The schools are too full of children. The restaurants are too full of eaters. If you try to go to see a doctor, you find the waiting-room full and a long line of people straggling down the hall. There's no room in the hospitals for the women who are going to have babies. 'So far we've been lucky,' the health officers say with terror in their voices, 'not to have had an epidemic. But we've got our fingers crossed.'

38 ★ James H. S. Bossard, "Family Backgrounds of Wartime Adolescents"

Migration was, of course, only one of several wartime changes that affected family stability. The ways in which economic prosperity, wartime anxiety, and social mobility influenced the relations of parents and adolescents were evaluated by James Bossard, a sociologist at the University of Pennsylvania. [The Annals of the American Academy of Political and Social Science, CCXLVI (November 1944), 33-42. Footnotes omitted. Reprinted by permission.]

So comprehensive and fundamental are the changes wrought by war, and so closely is the family interrelated with the larger society, that there is perhaps no aspect of family life unaffected by war. This article seeks to select and to analyze certain consequences which seem to have particular significance to civilian life, and for the family's adolescent members. Seven such aspects are selected for discussion. . . .

The War Rich

Considering the parents of contemporary adolescents, it is evident on the basis of age sequence that the depression decade was for many of them a trying period. The onset of the depression found them with children in arms; the low point of the depression saw these children at, or approaching, school age. To some of these parents wartime prosperity comes as the first financial windfall of their married life; to many it comes to lighten an anxiety over finances which was chronic or intermittent for a decade. To put the matter bluntly, much of the new "war money" has been going to families who have not had a good deal before, and how they react to this experience is a matter of great importance for the students of the family. Clearly enough, many of them, sobered by their recent experience, are using this new money wisely, as data on savings and the purchase of government bonds clearly indicate. Anticipation of postwar depression is widespread and there are many families who are seeking within their utmost limits to be prepared for it. Unfortunately there are others who are indulging in an orgy of spending, much of it unwisely. Never having had much money before, they seem now not to know what to do with it. Recalling the ages of the parents of our particular interest, one observes and hears of many who are indulging in a sort of last "middle-age fling" before the next stage of maturity overtakes them.

The War Poor

Over against the war-rich families there is a great mass of new or war poor. These are the families whose incomes are fixed, absolutely or relatively, such as teachers, public officials, clerks, and other varieties of white-collar workers. A subcommittee of the United States Senate, headed by Senator Elbert D. Thomas, estimates that more than twenty million Americans fall in this category. . . .

Families respond to these economic pressures in either or both of two ways. One is that of added effort, to increase the family income. This involves the acceptance of extra jobs, of added duty, and of overtime work, and the seeking of employment by additional members of the family, particularly the wife. The other device is that of economies in family expenditures, which shade from the elimination of nonessentials to a reduction of the family plane of living. It is the common experience of mankind that in the reduction of this type, children are likely to suffer somewhat disproportionately. . . .

Wartime Anxieties in Family Backgrounds

It is obvious that there are many developments in our culture during the present war which are productive of feelings of marked anxiety, tension, fear, apprehension, and the like. There are the demands of the Selective Service, uncertain at best and confused and bungled by varying degrees of ineptness in many areas; uncertainties concerning the whereabouts, the physical condition, and the mental health of family members or relatives in the service; apprehension over separations of families, for either military or employment purposes; feelings of insecurity concerning jobs and income, particularly, again, of those connected with the war effort; worriment over the darkening shadows of increasing income taxation and rising costs of living, especially in families with adolescents in school; concern over plans for the careers, school and work, of adolescents approaching the age of military service; uncertainty over the difficulties of securing such rational indispensables as fuel, meat, and the like. All of these and many others fit as perfectly as a tailored glove the psychiatrist's description of anxiety-producing conditions. Truly, wartime anxiety is a family problem of no mean proportions. Obviously, too, it is a background which breeds restlessness, defiance, emotional disturbance, and various other negative forms of behavior. . . .

War and the Time-Energy Requirement of Parenthood

There are many aspects of life in these wartime days that are making serious inroads upon the time and the energy of family members. For millions of mothers, housekeeping has become a far more exacting task. Rationing, shortages requiring shopping at several stores or on successive days, waiting lines in stores due to shortage of help, curtailment of delivery services—all these and other wartime developments not only increase the time but also the nervous energy involved in what is considered routine housework. Lack of servants throws homemaking duties on family members not accustomed to, and perhaps not qualified for, such tasks. Community and civic groups related to war work make added demands of all kinds. Many fathers and mothers have taken on additional jobs in order to meet the rising tide of taxes and living costs.

There is, to be sure, a reverse side to all this. The war has curtailed many activities which in former days tended to be disruptive of family life. Less gasoline and fewer cars have meant more family life in many homes; crowded traveling conditions have had the same effect. Life before the war was replete with many activities, both of parents and of adolescents, whose curtailment or disappearance during the war may represent a gain in many ways.

War and Parent-Adolescent Conflicts

Adolescence is a period both of inner turmoil and of outer conflict. Much of both is the result of certain strains and stresses in the relation between the adolescent and his family. . . .

War tends to aggravate and intensify these conflicts, and in many ways. First, war creates excitement. It arouses intense emotional stimuli in certain areas of life, and soon these come to be extended to other areas. One result is to foster activity. People feel the urge to do things, adolescents as well as parents. For adults, all kinds of socially approved avenues exist to channelize this stirring urge. Not so for adolescents. . . .

Second, war brings to adolescents increased opportunities to develop self-reliance and independence. Such are the wartime demands for labor that almost any young person near the legal age may secure a position. One meets these young people at work in the stores, on farms, in filling stations, in drug stores, at defense plants, doing odd jobs, earning their own wages, taking the place of adults. One feature of their employment calls for special comment. Many adolescents are getting wartime wages and they compare them with those earned by their parents several years ago during the depression. Young persons are neither economists nor philosophers; they simply make a comparison, and it is not to their own disadvantage. One may applaud or regret this premature independence as one will, but its reality and the relation of that reality to parent-child conflicts cannot be ignored. "The old man can't say nothin' ta me about comin' in late, I helps ta pay the rent." . . .

Another group of parent-adolescent conflicts, peculiarly important in the United States at the moment, grows out of the national origin of selected population elements. There are in the United States a large number of adolescents whose parents are of German, Italian, or Japanese origin. Some of these parents were born in these respective countries; others, born here, have retained the language and the mannerisms of the country of origin. Their children, on the other hand, are American born, American schooled, and American indoctrinated. In every respect they identify themselves with the United States, and to the extent and with the fervor that they so do, they tend to resent their parents, or at least the strain of their enemy-alien origin. Family situations of this kind create not only conflict but also many other problems, often very painful and prolonged.

Finally, war creates parent-adolescent conflicts through its acceleration of cultural change. Some part of the conflict between generations is the inevitable result of the time span between them and the changes which occur during this period. The young tend to accept the new; the middle-aged and the old incline toward the status quo. When the rate of cultural change is slow, the resultant cultural differences that develop between generations are relatively few and small; as the rate of change rises, the differences grow apace. The importance of war in this connection is that it precipitates and stimulates cultural changes on a broad scale. Sociologically speaking, war is a complex of social changes involving the entire societal pattern; one phase of this is to break the cultural continuities between generations, with an inevitable increase of conflicts between them.

War and Changes in the Family Structure

The family is, from one point of view, a structure. This means that it is an organization of constituent elements (i.e., persons) with continuing relationships between these elements. The nature, the composition, and the relationships of this structure have great significance for the adolescent because they constitute the over-all framework within which the interactive and cultural processes of the family operate. It is one of the costs of war that it results in many modifications or mutilations of the family structure through its removal, temporarily or permanently, of members of the family group. Such removals, most frequent in the homes of adolescents in this war, include fathers and older brothers and sisters. . . .

Family Migrations and the Adolescent

War redistributes population. Complicating all the problems of American families today is the fact that millions of them have moved from their customary locale to follow the call of war-production jobs. This huge reshuffling of the national population is significant in many ways: we are concerned here with its meaning for the family backgrounds of wartime adolescents.

Migrant war workers, or "defense workers" as they are generally called, have a rather distinctive status in the communities to which they have come. They tend to be spoken of as "those families who are here on defense jobs," with an implication that they are fly-by-night sort of folks. In many areas they are resented because they overtax living, schooling, and recreational facilities already strained. In other places they are crowded in trailer camps that may come to be regarded as a menace to the community. In some cities, like Detroit, they particularly accentuate housing conditions already quite bad. In other cases their status is complicated by the fact that they represent minority groups. Rather generally, older residents resent their use of community facilities to whose maintenance they have not contributed through taxation; they particularly resent their special privileges as defense workers in securing new automobiles and extra gasoline allotments. On the whole, and to a considerable extent, migrant war-working families live in war communities as strangers, objects of a rather pervasive social isolation.

This isolation of "defense families" is a very real factor in the lives of their adolescent members, for adolescence is the stage in life history when the chief emphasis is upon the development of group contacts outside the family. It is in this normal process, so important in the development of the personality, that the adolescent member of a war migrant family encounters the social isolation of his kind. This problem is real, serious, tragic.

Again, adolescents in migrant homes lack the feelings of security that come from living in familiar surroundings. Adults talk glibly of the ease with which young people make new contacts; extensive studies which I have made convince me that the security which the growing child obtains from living under circumstances and with persons which are familiar and established is of tremendous importance to his normal development. Moreover, the migrant family moves not only into strange surroundings, but often into a culture which is quite different from that of the family.

THE NEW ROLE OF WOMEN

No figure better illustrated the wartime changes in family life than "Rosie the Riveter." Indeed, millions of women went to work who would not have taken jobs in peacetime, and they often performed tasks that had traditionally been reserved to men. During the war, the number of women workers rose from 12 to 16.5 million; by mid-1945 women constituted 36 per cent of the civilian labor force. Many were employed in shipyards, aircraft factories, munitions plants, and other branches of industry. This employment naturally gave rise to problems relating to morale, division of labor, and seniority, but on the whole women proved to be efficient workers. While one New York City fashion designer claimed to have taken a job in a munitions plant for patriotic reasons ("To hell, I said, with the penthouse studio and cocktails and fashion shows. . . . This war is too damn serious, and it is too damn important to win it"), it seems clear that most women were motivated primarily by economic considerations.

39 ★ *Ethel Erickson,* "Women's Employment in the Making of Steel"

The Women's Bureau of the Department of Labor prepared a number of studies of working women. Often they were designed to show what kinds of jobs women did most efficiently and what modifications in personnel procedures their employment required. As this report makes clear, the employment of women in steel mills was limited by tradition and the hazardous nature of the work. [Bulletin of the Women's Bureau, No. 192-5, Washington, 1944, pp. 3-5, 19-20.]

Steelmaking traditionally has been men's business. Steelmaking is a heavy and dirty business and women workers have been taboo. Iron ore, coal, and limestone, the basic raw materials for steel, are earthy, bulky, and heavy. Steel mills spread over wide areas and intense heat and massive equipment are necessary in processing. These marked characteristics of the industry and inherent hazards have tended naturally to shut out women, with their lesser strength and endurance.

In peacetime about the only job within the mills on which women were found was sorting and inspecting tinplate. As assorters, women were considered more efficient than men in flipping the mirrored tin sheets, inspecting for surface flaws, grading and judging the thickness and weight with their touch sensitivity. As assorters, however, women have constituted only a fraction of 1 per cent of the employees in the steel industry. Women clerical workers, of course, have been employed in the administrative offices of the companies for many years, but plant-office and pencil jobs of a semiclerical nature within the mills were held almost exclusively by men.

Not until months after Pearl Harbor did the steel industry feel the shortage of manpower sufficiently to consider women as a source of labor for augmenting their force and replacing men. Steelmen—both managers and workers—generally did not welcome the advent of women into their mills and feared that women would not be able to do a full job and would be a disrupting element and liability. The heaviness of the raw materials, the weight of steel products, the massive equipment, the spatial spread, the heat, fumes, and hazards do not offer employment possibilities that normally would be considered desirable or attractive to women. Also, there was a deeply rooted prejudice and tradition against women workers in the steel mills similar to that which prevails in the mining industry.

During 1942 a small number of women began to appear in the laboratories and plant offices of some of the mills, and by the end of the year, in a few mills, there were women on the lighter cranes and on labor gangs around the yards. Most mills, however, did not take on women until 1943, and though by the closing months of 1943 women are working in most of the country's steel mills, their numbers and proportions are small and their utilization is restricted generally to the lighter and least skilled jobs. In some of the mills, however, they are found in almost every department. There are women working at the ore docks, in the storage yards for raw materials, on the coal and ore trestles, in the coke plants, the blast furnaces, the steel furnaces, the rolling mills, and the finishing mills that are doing fabricating on shells, guns, and regular products such as nails, spikes, and bolts. On the whole, management, realizing that much of the work requires strength or exposure to special hazards, has been cautious in the selection of jobs for women and has provided better service and welfare facilities for women than for men. In old mills, where working conditions are poorer than the prevailing standards, and service facilities are most meager for men, there has been less employment of women than in the more modern mills.

During the late summer and fall of 1943, agents of the Women's Bureau visited steel mills in the principal steel-producing areas. One mill in Colorado had been visited as early as May. The occupations of the women, the hours worked, rates of pay, working conditions, and other factors affecting their employment were included in the inquiry. Data on jobs filled by women were collected for 41 steel mills. The proportion of women in the total force in the 41 mills was 10.6 per cent, in the production areas 8.1 per cent, and in the administrative offices and on salaried pay rolls 35.2 per cent. The proportion of women in production work varied by plant from 3.2 per cent to 16.1 per cent. . . .

While all the major divisions of steelmaking have women employees, it seems true that the more closely a job is associated with the handling of basic raw materials, the less suitable the job is deemed to be for women. The ore docks, the receiving and storage yards, the coke and by-products plants, the blast furnaces and the steel furnaces—the open-hearth, Bessemer-converter, and electric furnaces—offer an extremely limited field for the employment of women and actually the proportion of the women in these divisions is small. In the rolling mills there are more possibilities of employing women, and there are still more in the fabricating and finishing divisions. The laboratories, the maintenance, service, and clerical divisions, with a large number of jobs that might be considered incidental rather than related directly to steelmaking, probably offer the most in possibilities for the effective utilization of women. The laboratories and plant offices seem to afford opportunities for their continued post-war employment. . . .

Women are now working in most divisions of the steel industry but their proportion is small, about 8 per cent. The need for new workers is at the labor level and most of the women are recruited at this classification. Some of the jobs that would seem most appropriate for women are closed to them because of the seniority system. In the basic processes of the blast furnaces and steel works, most of the jobs other than those of a labor classification expose the worker to high temperatures and other strains inherent in a heavy industry. The possibilities of employing any significant proportion of women in the preliminary processes seems slight.

More women are employed in the rolling mills and fabrication departments, but these too have more heavy jobs than light ones. The work in the laboratory and quality-control sections appears especially suitable for women, and this would seem to be a place where a large proportion of the force could be women in normal as well as in war times.

Women are not able to work where marked spurts of strength and energy are necessary at times. Most of the women are employed on the labor gangs or the auxiliary jobs, such as crane operator, crane follower, laboratory aide, inspector, controlman and pumpman tending levers and valves, and as general helpers in the maintenance divisions. Management does not anticipate that women will form any large proportion of the steel-mill workers, but more can be employed. To secure effective employment of women—most of whom are inexperienced—management has given and must continue to give consideration to the lesser strength, the lack of industrial experience and familiarity with heavy industry, and the short-time viewpoint of women's employment in the industry. It appears to be generally agreed that women's employment in steel is a temporary war expediency and that men returning from the armed services will have seniority and priority on the jobs in the industry after the war, so it seems hardly fair to ask women to do extremely heavy labor and dangerous jobs and dissipate their strength on employment that is of a temporary nature.

40 ★ *Dorothy K. Newman,* "Employing Women in Shipyards"

The Women's Bureau seemed proud of the ability demonstrated by women workers, yet fearful that widespread employment might be injurious to their well-being. This report pointed to the importance of protecting women shipyard workers by assigning tasks to them carefully, assuring them equal pay and opportunity for advancement, and providing adequate safety instruction. [Bulletin of the Women's Bureau, No. 192-6, Washington, 1944, pp. 1-6.]

Recent and Unprecedented Employment of Women

Just a little over 2 years ago the subject and purpose of this bulletin would have been considered as fanciful as a tale from the Arabian Nights. That American women should take active part in the man's job of building and repairing ships was almost inconceivable. As recently as July 1941 an outstanding periodical made sport of the extreme anti-feminine attitude of what is now one of the most publicized woman-employing ship building and repair corporations in the country. At that time, nearly 2 years after war began in Europe and but 5 months before Pearl Harbor, women were not accepted by the firm even as office secretaries, and the lone women telephone operators were, as it was facetiously reported, "kept under lock and key."

Times have changed with lightning speed. By late 1943, thousands of women along both coasts and on the Gulf, Great Lakes, and inland waterways were actively engaged in almost every phase of ship building and repair work, and it is anticipated that it will be necessary to recruit thousands more before the war is over. Though the introduction of women into the shipyards did not begin in earnest until the fall of 1942, by January 1943 as many as 4 per cent of all the production wage earners in the industry were women. The proportion had risen to a little over 5 per cent by March, and by September to 9.5 per cent. In January 1944 it was 10 per cent. These figures include the 8 navy yards engaged in ship construction and repair, in which women have made extensive gains and comprised in September nearly one-fourth of the women wage earners in the industry.

Many Adjustments Required in an Expanding Industry

The unprecedented influx of women into the shipyards has been the inevitable accompaniment of this country's tremendous war ship-building program, for which it has been necessary to recruit hundreds of thousands of additional workers since Pearl Harbor. The first 17 months of wartime production witnessed an increase of 189 per cent in shipyard personnel. Old-established yards employing from 3,000 to 10,000 workers in 1939 and 1940 had 5 to nearly 8 times that many late in 1943, and there are some shipyards for which ground had not even been broken in 1940 that employed 20,000 to 40,000 workers in the spring of 1943 when the peak had not yet been reached. Expansion on so gigantic a scale in competition with other war industries and Selective Service brought shipbuilders face to face with the necessity of employing women to help to produce the enormous tonnage so urgently needed.

Such rapid development alone carries with it innumerable problems of administration and plant adjustment, but coupled with the necessity for drawing on a labor element never before tried in the industry, the problems became extremely numerous and complex. Organized training programs had to be set up within the shipyards to provide instruction for the thousands of workers, men as well as women, who had never held tools before, much less seen a ship under construction. Special training was necessary for the supervisors who had never had so many workers under them, many having themselves only recently been promoted from the ranks. Rapid upgrading of men into the skilled and leadership jobs became a practical necessity for the most economical utilization of labor. As the nucleus of skilled and experienced workers has become dispersed and proportionately smaller, the training structure has grown in size and importance. In many yards now the training director helps to control the rate of accession and allocation of the labor force.

Personnel, medical, and safety programs have had to be enlarged and modified to accommodate the mass hiring, placement, and protection of inexperienced workers. Effective selection of thousands of employees in short periods of time has required careful study of procedures and change in methods and policies. Alarming turn-over and labor scarcity have resulted in the introduction in many places of transfer bureaus and exit interviewing.

If the administrative offices have been affected by the magnitude of the war shipbuilding program, those planning and supervising the actual work have had to make even more fundamental and drastic adjustments. Under normal circumstances, ship construction is custom work; each vessel, whether a "sister ship" or one of a kind, differs from every other in detail if not design and requires a complete set of templates of its own. Now, however, hundreds of ships of the same kind, particularly cargo vessels, are being made with standardized materials according to a single pattern. Consequently, mass-production techniques involving assembly-line and prefabrication methods have been sought and developed. Even in the case of the many ships that still are built to individual plan, the work has been broken down to meet the dearth of all-round craftsmen, thus allowing introduction and training of specialists to perform one part of a process, operate one machine, or concern themselves with but one section of the ship. Making all this more possible, the speedier and easier assembly technique of welding has almost replaced riveting wherever feasible and hand welding and burning are giving way to machine methods in some yards and on larger jobs. Automatic assembly fasteners are being used here and there instead of tack welding.

Such examples of the effect on the industry of the tremendously accelerated shipbuilding program could be multiplied. In their broader aspects most of the changes are similar to those made in other industries under like pressure. Many have eased the way for the employment of women, especially those changes developed to meet the need for training and employing inexperienced men in great numbers and for building many ships of the same design. Others, however, have been required only because women were employed.

Lack of Preparation for Women's Employment

But the need to draw from the woman labor force often was not realized and accepted till the very last moment, leaving little time for study and planning. In many cases the management plunged headlong even before essential and obvious provision had been made to accommodate the newcomers. This was not surprising in view of acute manpower shortages in shipbuilding areas, yet it was nothing less than daring in an industry so bound in the tradition of dirt, sweat, and rough and tumble, so thoroughly male that any woman who ventured into a yard was greeted with hooting and whistling. The physical and administrative adaptations that should be introduced to insure women's efficient performance and necessary comfort on the job frequently are as nothing compared with the mental hurdles that must be overcome. Problems that are brought to the attention of those interested in women's success often stem as much from attitudes toward women workers in the man's world of shipbuilding as from the actual situation. Yet women frequently were taken on before the human or psychological adaptations necessary to avoid confusion, discontent, and waste, much less the physical and sometimes administrative changes necessary, had been attempted.

When field representatives of the Women's Bureau made visits to 41 shipyards between the beginning and the early fall of 1943, few yards had employed women for as long as a year; many had begun hiring women to do production work only a few months before; 6 had not yet hired any women for production work. Though the yards with women workers still were feeling their way, over half already were employing hundreds of women, some of them thousands, and in many cases expecting to hire hundreds or thousands more. While building more ships than ever before and servicing the Fleet, not a few were functioning under inadequate arrangements, hoping gradually to arrive at a satisfactory solution of their personnel problems with women. To be sure, some had already made excellent progress. Most had forged ahead in at least some phases, such as securing good safety observance, satisfactory rest- and wash-room facilities, and productively efficient distribution of the women on jobs; others were struggling with these aspects of the situation but had mastered other aspects. Many, aware of inadequacies, sought advice. Women's Bureau field representatives were asked in several of the yards visited to submit formal recommendations based on analysis and study of individual yard conditions and problems.

It is clear, then, that the shipyards are charting new seas in the utilization of the woman labor force, and the mistakes or successes that result may have a profound effect not only on the production and repair of ships, but on the cost and efficiency of such production and the health, work, and life histories of thousands of women. It is important to take stock now. Misconceptions should be dispelled, well-

founded facts pooled, and the fund of information available from industries with longer histories in the employment of women disseminated.
It is with these objects in view that the present report is submitted. It is
the aim of the Women's Bureau through the recommendations and suggestions made here to promote conditions for the woman shipyard
worker conducive to her most efficient and productive employment and
her well-being as a member of society and the labor force. . . .

1. Secure the cooperation of men supervisors and workers.
2. Select and place women carefully.
3. Employ women only in jobs found to be suitable.
4. Pay women and upgrade them on the same basis as men.
5. Schedule an 8-hour day and a 48-hour 6-day week; allow a lunch
   period of at least 30 minutes, and rest periods of 10 to 15 minutes in
   each work spell of as much as 4 hours. Rotate shifts no more frequently than every two months.
6. Set up an effective woman employee counselor system.
7. Give new women workers preliminary induction into the work and
   environment of the shipyard before putting them on the job.
8. Provide personal-service, food, and medical facilities that meet approved standards of adequacy and quality.
9. Study and expand the safety program to adapt it to women workers,
   and instruct women thoroughly in safe work practice.

YOUTH AND THE WAR

Unprecedented family mobility, wide-
spread employment of women, and the prolonged absence of fathers
called to service all had disturbing effects upon American children.
Youngsters left to fend for themselves after school—"latchkey children"
or "eight-hour orphans"—caused concern. In addition, the war changed
the lives of many adolescents. Between 1940 and 1944, the number of
teenagers attending school declined by 1.25 million, and most who left
school took jobs. As a result, the long-term trend toward a reduction of
child labor was temporarily reversed. The number of teenage workers
rocketed from 1 to 2.9 million; four times as many fourteen- and fifteen-
year-old girls were working at the end of the war than at its start. Community leaders predicted that economic independence, family disruption,
and wartime anxiety would lead to a growth of delinquency; but while
some increase in juvenile crime occurred, it appears that these fears were

largely unfounded. The war may have had damaging psychological effects upon some young people, but it does not seem that delinquent behavior was the result.

41 ★ *Ella A. Merrit and Floy Hendricks,* "Trend of Child Labor"

Although many child workers were among the social casualties of war, most teenagers who worked did so out of choice, not necessity, and received wages which permitted some sense of economic independence. The following account of the effect of war upon child labor was written by officials of the U.S. Children's Bureau. [Monthly Labor Review, LX (April 1945), 756-61, 770-75. Footnotes omitted.]

The war years from 1940 to 1944 have radically changed the picture of child labor and youth employment in the United States. In the two decades preceding 1940, the employment of boys and girls had been steadily decreasing. The number of working minors 14 through 17 years of age, as counted by the Census, fell from nearly 2½ millions in 1920 to about 1 million in 1940. During the 4 years since 1940, urgent demands for workers of all ages, especially in war production centers, the opening up of new job opportunities for children and young persons, high wartime wages, patriotic pressures, and social restlessness have pushed the numbers of employed boys and girls of this age group up to unprecedented levels. This upward swing in the number of teen-age workers has been clearly reflected in the three major sources of data on national trends in child labor and youth employment—the reports sent to the Children's Bureau on age or employment certificates required for children going to work, the records of young persons under 18 applying for social security account numbers, and United States Census figures.

Employment and age certificate reports, which show the trend in child labor from year to year rather than a cross section of the actual number of young persons employed at any given moment, indicate that more than seven times as many boys and girls aged 14 through 17 years entered the labor market in 1943 as in 1940 and went into work generally subject to Federal or State child-labor regulation. In States and cities reporting for each of these years, the number of minors 14 through 17 years of age who obtained certificates for full-time or part-time work increased from roughly 175,000 in 1940 to more than 1,320,000 in 1943. Preliminary data for 1944 indicate that in general the high level of 1943 is being maintained.

The record of applicants under 18 years of age for social security account numbers tells a similar story. From 1940 through 1943 the number of minors under 18 years of age applying for account numbers more than trebled, climbing from roughly 950,000 to 2,900,000. In 1944 there was a drop from 1943 to slightly over 2 millions; but despite this decrease the 1944 figure was more than twice as high as that for 1940.

Census figures for 1940 and estimates based on Census sample surveys since that date show an increase from about 1,000,000 in 1940 to nearly 3,000,000 in April 1944 in the number of young workers 14 through 17 years of age. During the summer months of 1943 and 1944 the number approached 5,000,000.

This wartime increase in child labor has meant a loss of education for children and an increase in illegal employment. According to the U.S. Office of Education figures, high-school enrollment had reached a total of 7,244,000 in the school year 1940-41 (an increase of nearly 5,000,000 since the school year 1919-20) whereas in 1943-44, three years later, the number of children enrolled had dropped by nearly 1,000,000.

Large increases in the extent of illegal employment have been noted by both State and Federal labor inspectors. For instance, in one State (North Carolina) there were 14 times as many child-labor law violations found by State inspectors in 1943 as in 1940 and 22 times as many in the first half of 1944 as in the first half of 1940; in another (Illinois), more than 500 establishments were found to be in violation in the first 6 months of 1944 as compared with fewer than 40 in the corresponding period of 1941; in a third (New York), there was a rise of nearly 400 per cent between 1940 and 1943 in the number of boys and girls under 18 found to be illegally employed. The figures for violations of the child-labor provisions of the Federal Fair Labor Standards Act, which are administered by the Children's Bureau, tell the same story as the record of violations of State laws. Nearly five times as many children (8,436) were found by inspectors to be illegally employed in the year ended June 30, 1944, as in the year ended June 30, 1941 (1,761), and these violations occurred in more than five times as many establishments (2,938) in the latter as in the former year (579).

These facts emphasize the need to reestablish and improve the legislative standards that help to give to the country's youth opportunity for education and for normal physical and social development, and to strengthen the machinery for their enforcement. . . .

In general, child labor during the nineteen-twenties rose or fell along with general business conditions, though there was a total decrease particularly for the 14- and 15-year-old group as a result of improvement of child-labor and school-attendance standards. In the years between 1929 and 1943 new and more decisive factors entered into the situation. The period began with the onset of one of the worst depressions in this country's history. It ended with a new peak of employment and production induced by the war. The 15-year record of the numbers of employment certificates issued to young workers 14 through 17 years of age shows that the trend of youth employment followed the trend of general employment with two important exceptions when, twice in the decade and a half, Nation-wide legislation was enacted drastically affecting the employment of children under 16 years of age. In 1933 and 1934 the NRA codes, practically all of which included a 16-year minimum age requirement, reduced very materially the employment of young workers 14 and 15 years of age during the 2 years they were in effect. The removal of the code restrictions in 1935 was followed by an upward swing for employment of this younger group, which continued until it was checked by the slight economic recession beginning in 1937 and continuing into the first part of 1938. In October 1938 the Fair Labor Standards Act established a basic 16-year minimum age in industries producing goods for shipment in interstate commerce, with the result that in spite of rising employment the number of 14- and 15-year old children going to work continued to drop. The permanent decrease which this legal standard might have been expected to bring about, however, was almost immediately reversed by the heavy wartime demands for workers, although the law has been an effective barrier against wholesale employment of children under 16 in manufacturing industries. . . .

Using the year 1939 as a base, the index for total estimated non-agricultural employment rose from 100 to 131, whereas for minors 16 and 17 years of age obtaining employment certificates the index rose from 100 to 592 and that for children 14 and 15 years of age soared from 100 to 1,184. . . .

War demands for labor and new types of job openings have brought about a great change in the industries and occupations entered by young workers obtaining certificates. In general the trend for 14- and 15-year-olds has been away from the typical "children's occupations," such as errand work, street trades, and housework as the major type of work, into employment in retail stores and wholesale establishments, and for the 16- and 17-year-olds away from the trade and miscellaneous service industries into various types of employment in manufacturing and mechanical establishments.

42 ★ *Katherine F. Lenroot,* Juvenile Delinquency

Katherine F. Lenroot, Chief of the Children's Bureau in the Department of Labor, submitted the following statement to a Senate investigating committee in November, 1943. Her discussion of the forces which contributed to juvenile delinquency and to a relaxation of moral standards echoed the apprehension of many who were concerned with the problems of youth. [*Wartime Health and Recreation,* Hearings before a subcommittee of the Committee on Education and Labor, U.S. Senate, Part I, Washington, 1944, pp. 100-15.]

Delinquency is a problem that is not readily susceptible to accurate and complete statistical measurement. Certain difficulties are readily apparent. It is not possible to determine the exact extent to which the increase in delinquency cases represents actual increase or to what extent it represents greater community concern, causing greater emphasis on finding cases and on taking measures that heretofore might not have been taken. It is unquestionable that emphasis placed on the control of venereal disease has resulted in the attention of the courts being called more frequently to problems of young girls than was formerly the case. Furthermore, from the standpoint of community concern about juvenile delinquency, the many unhappy, maladjusted, and neurotic children who fail to come to the attention of agencies and courts, yet who make up a large group of individuals who are potential delinquents, easily precipitated into delinquency by unfavorable environment, are of importance equal to those already delinquent in the legal sense.

Although we may lack the means of comprehensive measurement of the problem of delinquent behavior, evidence of increases during the past few years is apparent in recent reports from varied and reliable sources. Field reports of representatives of the Children's Bureau of the United States Department of Labor and other public and private agencies, and special studies and reports of particular communities indicate that the problem is of sufficient proportions to warrant concern.

Causal Factors

In wartime, as in peacetime, juvenile delinquency results from our failure to satisfy the basic needs of children and young people—the need for knowing that they are loved and cared for—the chance to take part as equals in school and recreational activities. The home and community through which these needs are met find their task more difficult by the dislocations they are undergoing in wartime.

Some of the wartime conditions which mean that homes and communities are not meeting the needs of children as well as they formerly did include the following:

Fathers are separated from their families because they are serving in the armed forces or working in distant war industries.

Mothers in large numbers are engaged in full-time employment and are therefore absent from the home most of the day.

An increasing number of children are now employed, in many instances under unwholesome conditions that impede their growth, limit their educational progress, or expose them to moral hazards.

The widespread migration of families to crowded centers of war industry has uprooted children from familiar surroundings and subjected them to life in communities where resources are overtaxed by the increased population.

Dance halls, beer parlors, and other attractions that flourish in industrial centers and near military establishments, unless kept under community control, frequently exert a harmful influence on youth.

The general spirit of excitement and adventure aroused by war, and the tension, anxiety, and apprehension felt by parents or other adults are reflected in restlessness, defiance, emotional disturbance, and other negative forms of behavior on the part of children and young people.

Conditions affecting children and young people in war-affected communities are conducive to lack of parental responsibility and resultant neglect and delinquency of children. In a report from a child-welfare worker in a southwestern State it was stated that several mothers who had followed their soldier husbands to a military camp secured work as waitresses or taxi dancers in the night cafes and left their children alone in hotel rooms without supervision. It is not surprising that such children, without protection of a secure home life, find it easy to drift into delinquency.

A typical situation reported by child-welfare workers as occurring in communities near Army camps is illustrated by the story of Julia, a 14-year-old girl found living with her girl friend aged 15, who was the wife of a soldier at the nearby camp. Both of the girls were having many soldiers visit them each night and were picked up by the police in one of the taverns near the camp. Julia told the child-welfare worker of her unhappy home situation in a dull little village in an adjoining State. She thought hitchhiking was fun and life around an Army camp exciting.

The type of community conditions which contribute to delinquency is pictured in the following excerpt from a special report made in a southern city located near a military camp:

"On either side of the road, a few feet apart, are gray framed structures, each identical to the next, with three rooms in a row. Each houses at least two families. A bed is visible from each open, unscreened front door. Forty to fifty per cent of the gross income of the inhabitants of these shacks goes to rent. The houses have never known paint; the yards, no planting. There is evidently overcrowding because of the large number of people of all ages sitting on steps and in the yards. All are barefooted. The yards are filled with garbage, watermelons, and a few sprigs of grass. Ragged white laundry is slung over fences and porch rails. The children are sitting idly or playing among all this."

The above description is typical of many situations where thousands of children are living in trailer camps, in shacks, and in overcrowded homes. Families and young girls especially flock to communities to be near the servicemen. Often the war worker brings his family into already crowded areas. Two or three families living in one apartment and the lack of privacy resulting; children in trailer camps without adequate play space; and the lack of stores and other essential community resources add to the general tensions of family life. Although war-housing projects have alleviated crowded housing conditions, community living also requires more than mere shelter. It includes indoor and outdoor play space, accessible schools, churches, and stores. When decent housing and adequate community services are present, the dangers of juvenile delinquency decrease.

The difficulties faced by school authorities in many war-affected communities, in making proper educational provision for increased numbers of children, should be mentioned as a factor closely related to the present delinquency problem. Reports from some of these communities show that the school enrollment has increased out of all proportion to available buildings, teachers, and equipment. Such conditions obviously affect the adjustment of children and seriously limit the positive contribution which the school can make to prevention of delinquency. This is an important consideration in relation to the fact that most juvenile delinquents are of school age.

The War Production Board established (January 3, 1942) the criterion of 200-per cent use of school buildings before critical materials could be used in the construction of additional classrooms. This results in double sessions or vastly crowded schools. The unfortunate result of double sessions can be seen in children wandering the streets and hanging around poolrooms and popular "hang outs." Many of these young people are living under boom-town conditions, in crowded housing, with both parents employed, thus eliminating the control of both the home and the school. Immediate and long-time effects of such conditions upon children and young people cannot be measured in terms of essential materials.

Employment of Mothers

A factor of major proportion in the cause of delinquency is the employment of mothers outside the home. The number of children requiring child-care services because their mothers are employed is constantly mounting. Some five and a half million women with children under 14 years of age were working outside their homes in April 1943, about 1,000,000 more than the number so employed in 1942. It was estimated that at least a million more workers would be employed this year and that most of them will have to come from the ranks of housewives, which will increase the number of children for whom care will be needed.

Inadequate provision for the care of children of working mothers constitutes an outstanding example of failure to meet children's wartime needs in a comprehensive way, adapted to the varying ages and circumstances of the children involved. Because the problem was created by war needs for women workers, chiefly in areas where shortage of school facilities and other factors have made the needs of children in the general population acute, assistance by the Federal Government, with detailed planning and administrative responsibility vested in State departments and local communities, was indicated. But there has been lack of clearcut and consistent policy, failure to recognize the legal and social responsibilities of the States, and failure to develop throughout the Nation comprehensive and sound community plans that would insure a differentiated program, built upon natural neighborhood ties and community resources, and would relate child-care services to an advisory and counseling service furnishing a continuing link between the mothers and the planning and administration of child-care programs. . . .

Child Labor and Youth Employment

The great increase in both full-time and part-time employment of boys and girls has aspects which are significant in any consideration of delinquency problems. . . .

Although employment under proper controls and under satisfactory conditions may have constructive elements for some children, many are working in jobs, such as those in places where liquor is sold, cheap restaurants, dance halls, honky tonks, and juke joints in which prevailing conditions are harmful to young people and may be factors in leading some of them into delinquency. It was reported to the Children's Bureau that in a military camp area in a southern State, girls 13 to 14 years old have been found working from 4 in the afternoon to 12 at night in questionable places such as honky tonks.

Some types of employment in the refreshment and amusement industries such as bowling alleys constitute special social hazards to young people. In one large city in New York State, the school attendance officer stated that there were only three alleys in the city that did not sell liquor. Many boys and girls are working for long hours and late at night—sometimes until 2 or 3 a. m. When employed late at night, they often are released in groups and in seeking recreation for themselves after work, drift into situations that contribute to delinquency. An example of this is found in the report of 3 boys in an eastern city who went into a drinking place on the way home from work in a bowling alley and became intoxicated. In another State some 12- and 13-year-old boys were brought before the court for stealing tires at 2 a. m. when on their way home from work in a bowling alley.

Much of this type of employment is contrary to the laws which in many States prohibit employment of children under 14 at any time or under 16 at night, and in many States prohibit employment under 16 or under 18 in places where liquor is sold. State departments of labor are seriously understaffed, and furthermore such illegal employment of minors is in scattered places of employment, where inspection and enforcement is particularly difficult.

Many of the children employed in these occupations are school children. Often they are so fatigued by the late night hours that they fall asleep in school. Or too tired to try to keep up the double burden of school and work, they become truants and thus start on the path to delinquency. Attendance officers find difficulty in coping with the problem, as they are carrying much heavier burdens than in the past because schools are overcrowded and children are tempted to drop out of school to take jobs with high wages. Many problems are created both for themselves and the community by the number of boys and girls who are migrating for jobs to war production centers, with or without their families.

43 ★ *Fritz Redl,* "Zoot Suits: An Interpretation"

During the war, some young men in large cities took to wearing zoot-suits—broad felt hats, wide trousers, long key chains, pocket knives and, according to one observer, hair "of increasing density and length at the neck." Zoot-suiters spent a good deal of time jitterbugging. In 1943, brawls between Mexican-American zoot-suiters and sailors occurred in Los Angeles. The city council tried to outlaw wearing zoot-suits, but as social psychologist Fritz Redl pointed out, the cult fulfilled important functions for its followers. [Survey Midmonthly, LXXIX (October 1943), 259-62. Reprinted by permission of Mrs. Helen Hall Kellogg.]

Who are the zoot suiters? Frankly—we do not know. But we can warn against premature generalizations. Most people seem to be more eager to "label" the phenomenon, than to find out what it is like. They call it either "Negro" or "typically delinquent" or what not. The only statements I can venture on the basis of our observations are:

Racially the phenomenon is not confined to the Negroes. In Detroit there are white zoot suit groups, especially some among the Italians. However, it does seem to be true that the majority of zoot suiters are Negroes. Remembering the Los Angeles incidents we should probably say: While not confined to minority groups, the zoot suit phenomenon draws its adherents from that group which the town is most conscious of as being a "minority."

Socio-economically we can say the zoot suit cult has penetrated to some extent among middle class youth. However, the mainsprings of the movement are obviously located in those socio-economic spheres which constituted the relief clientele and unemployed groups before the war. Warner and his crowd would describe the socio-economic status of most of the zoot suiters as "lower-lower to upper-lower." You remember that these classifications are not mainly meant to describe economic status but to signify sets of behavior and life-code. Young people in these groups would not buy or wear a tuxedo, even if they had the money to do so. But, of course, there are many persons who would not buy a tuxedo who are strongly identified with middle class standards, and would definitely reject the zoot suit philosophy. Maybe this description hits it closer: The zoot suit youngsters are found among those whose parents have experienced long years of unemployment and deprivation from security; now suddenly able to make some money on their own they are sure that this will not last long nor buy them acceptance in a middle class society.

Developmentally the picture is easier to draw. It includes the older adolescent and the younger adult, the age range being for the most part between sixteen and twenty-five. Girls as well as boys can be zoot suiters, if the term is used loosely to describe a type. And yet—the group formational elements which are inherent in the phenomenon are definitely carried by the male. The girls do not form into gangs. They play the role of either the dance partner or a part similar to the one the gangsters' girls play within a gang. It is puzzling to notice that all the cultist formality of clothing is concentrated on the boys' suits. The girls' outfit—sweater and skirt—is much more simple, inconspicuous, and functional.

What do they get out of it? It seems to me that I can differentiate between four types of zoot suiters:

1. *Those for whom the zoot suit is part of an expressional dance cult.* For a large number of zoot suiters, boys as well as girls, "jitterbugging" is something very serious indeed. They perform their dance with tribal fanaticism, with a high degree of absorption and devotion visible in their execution. Far from looking for trouble, these youngsters are most happy if they are let alone by neighborhood gangs. Nor do they care much whether they are "understood" by the adult. There is no doubt, however, that they "mean it." Just what it is that gets expression in these orgiastic performances or why it assumes this grotesque form would be hard to tell. All I know is that the cheap explanations of envious and indignant critics are way off the real mystery.

It is interesting, by the way, that the most serious jitterbugs are to be found among the Negro youth. These young Negroes are almost "cult conscious" about their performance. They have a deep contempt of the white groups who imitate the form of their dance without really getting the "spirit" of it. In fact, some of them accuse the whites of performing it in such a way that it not only loses its real "stuff," but becomes "dirty."

For all these dance enthusiasts, the zoot suit itself is only secondary. It is something like a cultist's robe, symbolizing their "belief" and separating them from those who do not share their semi-devotional experiences. Their dance is anything but a "delinquent" activity. It is the one serious enthusiasm that gives their life consistency and meaning. I am sure that it is an excellent mental hygiene device to help them in the

complicated task of growing up where they live—a much more significant device than any mental hygienist could have invented.

2. *Those for whom the zoot suit is a declaration of independence.* The
youngsters in this group, too, talk about and perform the dance of the
jitterbugs. Yet, their great moment is not experienced on the dance
floor. It comes over them when they walk in the streets, in their exciting
outfit. They thrive on the glances of awed admiration, of amused be-
wilderment, of indignant aversion, of open ridicule and hostility which
they reap wherever they go. Their knowledge that most "non-zoot
suiters" are against them is about all the unity they have so far achieved
among themselves. Their satisfaction does not reach orgiastic climaxes as
does that of the dance adepts. It is rather diffuse, distributed all over the
place. They reap it in instalments, through the constant stage of chronic
irritation among people whom they are happy to irritate. Their fun is
somewhat similar to the fun the college girl has when running around the
campus in slacks against dormitory rules. For this group the zoot suit
itself swallows up all the devotion and enthusiasm which others put into
the dance. They would even rather lose a job, than compromise in a
cowardly way with the drab demands of officially recognized clothing. . . .

3. *Those for whom it is the uniform of a spontaneous Youth Movement.*
A youngster belonging to either group thus far described still remains
an individualist. The zoot suit is *his* suit, the pleasure he gets out of it is
the pleasure it has for *him*. The revolt he seeks is against people *he*
knows or passes in the street, whose indignation about his behavior forms
his daydreams. Other zoot suiters mean little to him, except occasionally
in terms of reassurance. But there is another type of youngster for whom
the zoot suit is more than a provision for individual feelings of adolescent revolt. For this youngster the zoot suit is representative of something very much like a genuine and spontaneous youth movement. . . .
   The youngsters of this spontaneous movement are *not* delinquent.
They are normal, growing youngsters. They are tough and increase their
toughness under the impact of adolescent growth confusion and of the
socio-economic area in which their adolescence happens to occur—one
which demands toughness for survival. It is true that in the pursuit of
this type of "group life" these adolescents will often get into trouble
with the powers that have the task, to establish order. It is also true that,
because of the tough guy hero ideal, acts of violence and destruction will

occur, which, legally, can no doubt be termed as delinquent. It is not true, however, that this type of zoot suiter is a delinquent character. His delinquent acts are the consequence rather than the cause of what he is and represents. He is basically neither abnormal nor disturbed.

In reports, the "destruction" which happens in connection with zoot suit scandals is usually described in such a way that the element of "wantonness" or "senselessness" is emphasized. This characteristic is often a cause of surprise and wonder to the adult. It is, however, the one fact which is most clearly explained. These youngsters have no special goal-directed "gripe" at any one person or institution—certainly not against the very dance hall in which they had all the fun in the evening before they started cutting the plush seats to pieces. They only have loads of destructive urges, plus a general tendency to assert themselves as different from children and adults. The two elements together produce a similar phenomenon with which we are all very familiar: the college boy who cuts up for a few years after rather prolonged submission to adult stand-ards and before submersion into them for life. The zoot suiters come closer to the psychology of college boys than any other group. If you could change the socio-economic surroundings in which the two phe-nomena happen, the differences would tend to merge. It is not because the two groups are inherently so different, but because the place in which they live gives events such a different turn and meaning, that we fail to see the similarity. Thus we get disgusted and scared by the events themselves rather than trying to see what they mean after re-translation into the terms of adolescent psychology.

In calling the zoot suiters of type 3 a "genuine and spontaneous youth movement," I differentiated them from two other phenomena: political movements which are really adult, but happen to enroll youth among their membership; and educational group movements planned for youth by adults. On this basis it may be interesting to realize that the zoot suiters are *the only existing spontaneous youth movement* there is in this country, or what comes close to one. They are very different in their nature from anything like political or social or even racial youth groups with a planned philosophy and adult directed action, and they are just as different from organizations like the Boy Scouts, YMCA, or settlements and other social agencies for the domestication of youth. . . .

4. *Those for whom the zoot suit is a disguise for delinquent gang forma-tion.* There is no doubt that the zoot suit craze is also being used as a welcome disguise for delinquent gang formation. Thus, some of the old

neighborhood gangs of delinquent or semi-delinquent characters are now running around in zoot suits molesting non-zoot suiters or other zoot suit groups, or carrying out organized delinquent activity. In some areas there are zoot suit gangs who have a specified drugstore for a hangout, a secret code, an elaborate relay system so as to bring aid to affiliated subgroups that are in danger. In short, they are organized like any gang of delinquents. Some of these young gangsters may also be genuinely interested zoot suiters, just as some of them may also be interested in model airplanes, like to go dancing, or belong to some other club.

To describe the nature of these delinquent, organized gangs as though it was characteristic of the zoot suit phenomenon would be about as silly as to describe the activities of a stamp collector's club and to call them characteristic of the church to which its members happen to belong. The fact is that the zoot suit phenomenon, with its clothing fad, makes a convenient disguise for organizers of delinquent activity, but this does not mean that delinquency is characteristic of the phenomenon itself.

In short: The delinquency problem is a separate problem. The phenomenon of zoot suit activities and its influence on the psychology of adolescents from low income strata is another problem. In some points, the two overlap. Aside from that, they are distinctly different and the one cannot be solved or even understood through the other. Delinquent gangs who happen to wear zoot suits are still—delinquent gangs. And growing adolescents under certain socio-economic and psychological conditions will enjoy walking around in zoot suits. They are still growing adolescents with a special psychological problem to work out that way. To label them all delinquents or to refer to the zoot suit phenomenon as a simple "cause" for the delinquency problem is nothing but self deception.

6 The Quest for Meaning

THE DEBATE OVER WAR AIMS

The war may have crippled isolationism, but debate over the extent of America's world responsibilities in the postwar period continued. "Internationalism" was subject to divergent interpretations; its advocates disagreed as to the purpose of American involvement in the war and the nature of the peace that would follow. One group, including Henry Wallace and Sumner Welles, subscribed to the Wilsonian tenets of liberal internationalism. They hoped that the war would usher in a period of worldwide social reform and believed that peace should be founded on the equality of all nations. Other internationalists, for whom Walter Lippmann was an articulate spokesman, contended that this was an overly idealistic view. Americans, they reasoned, should understand the limitations upon world order imposed by nationalism, and recognize that peace could be attained only by agreement among the big powers. Franklin Roosevelt, who ordinarily set forth war aims in less utopian terms than had Wilson, selected "War of Survival" as the most appropriate term for the conflict. The President, however, tried to steer a middle course, recognizing that too blunt an assertion of realism might alienate public opinion, whereas too idealistic a stance might arouse expectations that could not be fulfilled.

44 ★ Henry R. Luce, "The American Century"

Henry R. Luce, a Willkie Republican, was publisher of Time, Life, *and* Fortune. *In February, 1941, more than nine months before the attack on Pearl Harbor, he published an editorial asserting that "America is in the war" even though peace "technically" existed. "We want Hitler stopped—more than we want to stay out of the war. So, at the moment, we're in." Luce admitted that the huge debt, swollen bureaucracy and increased executive authority required by war might prove dangerous,*

but explained why involvement could provide an opportunity for the
United States to exert its proper influence in the world. [The American
Century by Henry R. Luce, excerpts from an editorial which appeared
in *Life*, February 17, 1941, copyright © Time Inc. 1941. Reprinted by
permission.]

. . . In 1919 we had a golden opportunity, an opportunity unprecedented in all history, to assume the leadership of the world—a
golden opportunity handed to us on the proverbial silver platter. We
did not understand that opportunity. Wilson mishandled it. We rejected
it. The opportunity persisted. We bungled it in the 1920's and in the
confusions of the 1930's we killed it.

To lead the world would never have been an easy task. To revive
the hope of that lost opportunity makes the task now infinitely harder
than it would have been before. Nevertheless, with the help of all of
us, Roosevelt must succeed where Wilson failed.

The 20th Century Is the American Century
. . . Some Facts About Our Time

. . . This 20th Century is baffling, difficult, paradoxical, revolu-
tionary. But by now, at the cost of much pain and many hopes deferred,
we know a good deal about it. And we ought to accommodate our outlook to this knowledge so dearly bought. For example, any true conception of our world of the 20th Century must surely include a vivid
awareness of at least these four propositions.

First: our world of 2,000,000,000 human beings is for the first time
in history one world, fundamentally indivisible. Second: modern man
hates war and feels intuitively that, in its present scale and frequency,
it may even be fatal to his species. Third: our world, again for the first
time in human history, is capable of producing all the material needs of
the entire human family. Fourth: the world of the 20th Century, if it
is to come to life in any nobility of health and vigor, must be to a
significant degree an American Century.

As to the first and second: in postulating the indivisibility of the
contemporary world, one does not necessarily imagine that anything
like a world state—a parliament of men—must be brought about in this
century. Nor need we assume that war can be abolished. All that it is
necessary to feel—and to feel deeply—is that terrific forces of magnetic
attraction and repulsion will operate as between every large group of

human beings on this planet. Large sections of the human family may be effectively organized into opposition to each other. Tyrannies may require a large amount of living space. But Freedom requires and will require far greater living space than Tyranny. Peace cannot endure unless it prevails over a very large part of the world. Justice will come near to losing all meaning in the minds of men unless Justice can have approximately the same fundamental meanings in many lands and among many peoples.

As to the third point—the promise of adequate production for all mankind, the "more abundant life"—be it noted that this is characteristically an American promise. It is a promise easily made, here and elsewhere, by demagogues and proponents of all manner of slick schemes and "planned economies." What we must insist on is that the abundant life is predicated on Freedom—on the Freedom which has created its possibility—on a vision of Freedom under Law. Without Freedom, there will be no abundant life. With Freedom, there can be.

And finally there is the belief—shared let us remember by most men living—that the 20th Century must be to a significant degree an American Century. This knowledge calls us to action now.

America's Vision of Our World
. . . How It Shall Be Created

What can we say and foresee about an American Century? It is meaningless merely to say that we reject isolationism and accept the logic of internationalism. What internationalism? Rome had a great internationalism. So had the Vatican and Genghis Khan and the Ottoman Turks and the Chinese Emperors and 19th Century England. After the first World War, Lenin had one in mind. Today Hitler seems to have one in mind—one which appeals strongly to some American isolationists whose opinion of Europe is so low that they would gladly hand it over to anyone who would guarantee to destroy it forever. But what internationalism have we Americans to offer?

Ours cannot come out of the vision of any one man. It must be the product of the imaginations of many men. It must be a sharing with all peoples of our Bill of Rights, our Declaration of Independence, our Constitution, our magnificent industrial products, our technical skills. It must be an internationalism of the people, by the people and for the people.

In general, the issues which the American people champion revolve around their determination to make the society of men safe for the freedom, growth and increasing satisfaction of all individual men. Beside that resolve, the sneers, groans, catcalls, teeth-grinding, hisses and roars of the Nazi Propaganda Ministry are of small moment.

Once we cease to distract ourselves with lifeless arguments about isolationism, we shall be amazed to discover that there is already an immense American internationalism. American jazz, Hollywood movies, American slang, American machines and patented products, are in fact the only things that every community in the world, from Zanzibar to Hamburg, recognizes in common. Blindly, unintentionally, accidentally and really in spite of ourselves, we are already a world power in all the trivial ways—in very human ways. But there is a great deal more than that. America is already the intellectual, scientific and artistic capital of the world. Americans—Midwestern Americans—are today the least provincial people in the world. They have traveled the most and they know more about the world than the people of any other country. America's worldwide experience in commerce is also far greater than most of us realize.

Most important of all, we have that indefinable, unmistakable sign of leadership: prestige. And unlike the prestige of Rome or Genghis Khan or 19th Century England, American prestige throughout the world is faith in the good intentions as well as in the ultimate intelligence and ultimate strength of the whole American people. We have lost some of that prestige in the last few years. But most of it is still there.

No narrow definition can be given to the American internationalism of the 20th Century. It will take shape, as all civilizations take shape, by the living of it, by work and effort, by trial and error, by enterprise and adventure and experience.

And by imagination!

As America enters dynamically upon the world scene, we need most of all to seek and to bring forth a vision of America as a world power which is authentically American and which can inspire us to live and work and fight with vigor and enthusiasm. And as we come now to the great test, it may yet turn out that in all our trials and tribulations of spirit during the first part of this century we as a people have been painfully apprehending the meaning of our time and now in this moment of testing there may come clear at last the vision which will guide us to the authentic creation of the 20th Century—our Century.

Consider four areas of life and thought in which we may seek to realize such a vision:

First, the economic. It is for America and for America alone to determine whether a system of free economic enterprise—an economic order compatible with freedom and progress—shall or shall not prevail in this century. We know perfectly well that there is not the slightest chance of anything faintly resembling a free economic system prevailing in this country if it prevails nowhere else. What then does America have to decide? Some few decisions are quite simple. For example: we have to decide whether or not we shall have for ourselves and our friends freedom of the seas—the right to go with our ships and our ocean-going airplanes where we wish, when we wish and as we wish. The vision of America as the principal guarantor of the freedom of the seas, the vision of America as the dynamic leader of world trade, has within it the possibilities of such enormous human progress as to stagger the imagination. Let us not be staggered by it. Let us rise to its tremendous possibilities. Our thinking of world trade today is on ridiculously small terms. For example, we think of Asia as being worth only a few hundred millions a year to us. Actually, in the decades to come Asia will be worth to us exactly zero—or else it will be worth to us four, five, ten billions of dollars a year. And the latter are the terms we must think in, or else confess a pitiful impotence.

Closely akin to the purely economic area and yet quite different from it, there is the picture of an American which will send out through the world its technical and artistic skills. Engineers, scientists, doctors, movie men, makers of entertainment, developers of airlines, builders of roads, teachers, educators. Throughout the world, these skills, this training, this leadership is needed and will be eagerly welcomed, if only we have the imagination to see it and the sincerity and good will to create the world of the 20th Century.

But now there is a third thing which our vision must immediately be concerned with. We must undertake now to be the Good Samaritan of the entire world. It is the manifest duty of this country to undertake to feed all the people of the world who as a result of this worldwide collapse of civilization are hungry and destitute—all of them, that is, whom we can from time to time reach consistently with a very tough attitude toward all hostile governments. For every dollar we spend on armaments, we should spend at least a dime in a gigantic effort to feed the world—and all the world should know that we have dedicated our-

selves to this task. Every farmer in America should be encouraged to
produce all the crops he can, and all that we cannot eat—and perhaps
some of us could eat less—should forthwith be dispatched to the four
quarters of the globe as a free gift, administered by a humanitarian army
of Americans, to every man, woman and child on this earth who is really
hungry. . . .

But all this is not enough. All this will fail and none of it will
happen unless our vision of America as a world power includes a passionate devotion to great American ideals. We have some things in this
country which are infinitely precious and especially American—a love
of freedom, a feeling for the equality of opportunity, a tradition of self-
reliance and independence and also of co-operation. In addition to ideals
and notions which are especially American, we are the inheritors of all
the great principles of Western civilization—above all Justice, the love
of Truth, the ideal of Charity. The other day Herbert Hoover said
that America was fast becoming the sanctuary of the ideals of civilization. For the moment it may be enough to be the sanctuary of these
ideals. But not for long. It now becomes our time to be the powerhouse
from which the ideals spread throughout the world and do their mysterious work of lifting the life of mankind from the level of the beasts
to what the Psalmist called a little lower than the angels.

America as the dynamic center of ever-widening spheres of enterprise, America as the training center of the skillful servants of mankind,
America as the Good Samaritan, really believing again that it is more
blessed to give than to receive, and America as the powerhouse of the
ideals of Freedom and Justice—out of these elements surely can be
fashioned a vision of the 20th Century to which we can and will devote
ourselves in joy and gladness and vigor and enthusiasm. . . .

45 ★ Henry A. Wallace, "The Century of the Common Man"

*With this speech, delivered in May, 1942, Vice-President Henry A.
Wallace emerged as a leading exponent of liberal internationalism. The
talk also revealed the mystical and messianic character of Wallace's
thought. His major theme was taken up a few weeks later by Under-
Secretary of State Sumner Welles, who declared: "The principles of
the Atlantic Charter must be guaranteed to the world as a whole—in
all oceans and in all continents." More conservative elements in the
State Department, however, including Secretary Cordell Hull, regarded
Wallace and Welles as the "Post War Dream Boys." [From The Cen-*

tury of the Common Man, copyright, 1943, by Henry A. Wallace. Reprinted by permission of Harcourt, Brace & World, Inc.]

This is a fight between a slave world and a free world. Just as the United States in 1862 could not remain half slave and half free, so in 1942 the world must make its decision for a complete victory one way or the other.

As we begin the final stages of this fight to the death between the free world and the slave world, it is worth while to refresh our minds about the march of freedom for the common man. The idea of freedom —the freedom that we in the United States know and love so well—is derived from the Bible with its extraordinary emphasis on the dignity of the individual. Democracy is the only true political expression of Christianity.

The prophets of the Old Testament were the first to preach social justice. But that which was sensed by the prophets many centuries before Christ was not given complete and powerful political expression until our nation was formed as a Federal Union a century and a half ago. Even then, the march of the common people had just begun. Most of them did not yet know how to read and write. There were no public schools to which all children could go. Men and women can not be really free until they have plenty to eat, and time and ability to read and think and talk things over. Down the years, the people of the United States have moved steadily forward in the practice of democracy. Through universal education, they now can read and write and form opinions of their own. They have learned, and are still learning, the art of production—that is, how to make a living. They have learned, and are still learning, the art of self-government.

If we were to measure freedom by standards of nutrition, education and self-government, we might rank the United States and certain nations of Western Europe very high. But this would not be fair to other nations where education has become widespread only in the last twenty years. In many nations, a generation ago, nine out of ten of the people could not read or write. Russia, for example, was changed from an illiterate to a literate nation within one generation and, in the process, Russia's appreciation of freedom was enormously enhanced. In China, the increase during the past thirty years in the ability of the people to read and write has been matched by their increased interest in real liberty.

Everywhere, reading and writing are accompanied by industrial progress, and industrial progress sooner or later inevitably brings a strong labor movement. From a long-time and fundamental point of view, there are no backward peoples which are lacking in mechanical sense. Russians, Chinese, and the Indians both of India and the Americas all learn to read and write and operate machines just as well as your children and my children. Everywhere the common people are on the march. Thousands of them are learning to read and write, learning to think together, learning to use tools. These people are learning to think and work together in labor movements, some of which may be extreme or impractical at first, but which eventually will settle down to serve effectively the interests of the common man.

When the freedom-loving people march; when the farmers have an opportunity to buy land at reasonable prices and to sell the produce of their land through their own organizations, when workers have the opportunity to form unions and bargain through them collectively, and when the children of all the people have an opportunity to attend schools which teach them truths of the real world in which they live— when these opportunities are open to everyone, then the world moves straight ahead.

But in countries where the ability to read and write has been recently acquired or where the people have had no long experience in governing themselves on the basis of their own thinking, it is easy for demagogues to arise and prostitute the mind of the common man to their own base ends. Such a demagogue may get financial help from some person of wealth who is unaware of what the end result will be. With this backing, the demagogue may dominate the minds of the people, and, from whatever degree of freedom they have, lead them backward into slavery. Herr Thyssen, the wealthy German steel man, little realized what he was doing when he gave Hitler enough money to enable him to play on the minds of the German people. The demagogue is the curse of the modern world, and of all the demagogues, the worst are those financed by well-meaning wealthy men who sincerely believe that their wealth is likely to be safer if they can hire men with political "it" to change the signposts and lure the people back into slavery of the most degraded kind. Unfortunately for the wealthy men who finance movements of this sort, as well as for the people themselves, the successful demagogue is a powerful genie who, when once let out of his bottle, refuses to obey anyone's command. As long as his spell holds, he defies God Himself, and Satan is turned loose upon the world.

Through the leaders of the Nazi revolution, Satan now is trying to lead the common man of the whole world back into slavery and darkness. For the stark truth is that the violence preached by the Nazis is the devil's own religion of darkness. So also is the doctrine that one race or one class is by heredity superior and that all other races or classes are supposed to be slaves. The belief in one Satan-inspired Fuehrer, with his Quislings, his Lavals, and his Mussolinis—his "gauleiters" in every nation in the world—is the last and ultimate darkness. Is there any hell hotter than that of being a Quisling, unless it is that of being a Laval or a Mussolini?

In a twisted sense, there is something almost great in the figure of the Supreme Devil operating through a human form, in a Hitler who has the daring to spit straight into the eye of God and man. But the Nazi system has a heroic position for only one leader. By definition only one person is allowed to retain full sovereignty over his own soul. All the rest are stooges—they are stooges who have been mentally and politically degraded, and who feel that they can get square with the world only by mentally and politically degrading other people. These stooges are really psychopathic cases. Satan has turned loose upon us the insane.

The march of freedom of the past one hundred and fifty years has been a long-drawn-out people's revolution. In this Great Revolution of the people, there were the American Revolution of 1775, the French Revolution of 1792, the Latin American revolutions of the Bolivarian era, the German revolution of 1848, and the Russian Revolution of 1917. Each spoke for the common man in terms of blood on the battlefield. Some went to excess. But the significant thing is that the people groped their way to the light. More of them learned to think and work together.

The people's revolution aims at peace and not at violence, but if the rights of the common man are attacked, it unleashes the ferocity of a she-bear who has lost a cub. When the Nazi psychologists tell their master Hitler that we in the United States may be able to produce hundreds of thousands of planes, but that we have no will to fight, they are only fooling themselves and him. The truth is that when the rights of the American people are transgressed, as those rights have been transgressed, the American people will fight with a relentless fury which will drive the ancient Teutonic gods back cowering into their caves. The Götterdämmerung has come for Odin and his crew.

The people are on the march toward even fuller freedom than the most fortunate peoples of the earth have hitherto enjoyed. No Nazi counter-revolution will stop it. The common man will smoke the Hitler stooges out into the open in the United States, in Latin America, and in India. He will destroy their influence. No Lavals, no Mussolinis will be tolerated in a free world. . . .

We failed in our job after World War Number One. We did not know how to go about it to build an enduring worldwide peace. We did not have the nerve to follow through and prevent Germany from rearming. We did not insist that she "learn war no more." We did not build a peace treaty on the fundamental doctrine of the people's revolution. We did not strive whole-heartedly to create a world where there could be freedom from want for all the peoples. But by our very errors we learned much, and after this war we shall be in position to utilize our knowledge in building a world which is economically, politically and, I hope, spiritually sound.

Modern science, which is a by-product and an essential part of the people's revolution, has made it technologically possible to see that all of the people of the world get enough to eat. Half in fun and half seriously, I said the other day to Madame Litvinov: "The object of this war is to make sure that everybody in the world has the privilege of drinking a quart of milk a day." She replied: "Yes, even half a pint." The peace must mean a better standard of living for the common man, not merely in the United States and England, but also in India, Russia, China and Latin America—not merely in the United Nations, but also in Germany and Italy and Japan.

Some have spoken of the "American Century." I say that the century on which we are entering—the century which will come out of this war—can be and must be the century of the common man. Perhaps it will be America's opportunity to suggest the freedoms and duties by which the common man must live. Everywhere the common man must learn to build his own industries with his own hands in a practical fashion. Everywhere the common man must learn to increase his productivity so that he and his children can eventually pay to the world community all that they have received. No nation will have the God-given right to exploit other nations. Older nations will have the privilege to help younger nations get started on the path to industrialization, but there must be neither military nor economic imperialism. The methods of the nineteenth century will not work in the people's century which is now about to begin. India, China, and Latin America have a tremendous stake in the people's century. As their masses learn to read and write, and as they become productive mechanics, their standard of living will double and treble. Modern science, when devoted whole-

heartedly to the general welfare, has in it potentialities of which we do
not yet dream. . . .

No compromise with Satan is possible. We shall not rest until all
the victims under the Nazi yoke are freed. We shall fight for a complete
peace as well as a complete victory.

The people's revolution is on the march, and the devil and all his
angels can not prevail against it. They can not prevail, for on the side
of the people is the Lord.

He giveth power to the faint; to them that have no might He
increaseth strength . . .
They that wait upon the Lord shall mount up with wings as eagles;
they shall run, and not be weary; they shall walk and not be faint.

Strong in the strength of the Lord, we who fight in the people's cause
will never stop until that cause is won.

46 ★ *Wendell Willkie,* "One World"

*Until his death in 1944, the Republican 1940 presidential candidate
Wendell Willkie sought to lead his party toward an internationalist
position. In April, 1943, he published* One World, *an account of a
seven-week tour of Turkey, Russia, and China and of his discussions
with the leaders of those countries. Willkie discovered that a "deep
friendship" for the United States existed, and hoped that this "reservoir
of good will" could "be used to unify the peoples of the earth in the
human quest for freedom and justice." The book sold a million copies
within two months.* [One World *(New York: Simon and Schuster, Inc.,
1943), pp. 163-65, 171-87, 202-3. Reprinted by permission of Philip H.
Willkie.*]

It has become banal to say that this war is a revolution, in men's
thinking, in their way of living, all over the world. It is not banal to see
that revolution taking place, and that is what I saw. It is exciting and a
little frightening. It is exciting because it is fresh proof of the enormous
power within human beings to change their environment, to fight for
freedom with an instinctive, awakened confidence that with freedom
they can achieve anything. It is frightening because the different peoples
of the United Nations, let alone their leaders, have by no means reached
common agreement as to what they are fighting for, the ideas with
which we must arm our fighting men.

For, however important the role of bayonets and guns may have been in the development of mankind, the role of ideas has been vastly more important—and, in the long run, more conclusive. In historical times, at any rate, men have not often fought merely for the joy of killing each other. They have fought for a purpose. Sometimes that purpose has not been very inspiring. Sometimes it has been quite selfish. But a war won without a purpose is a war won without victory.

A most outstanding example of a war fought with a purpose was our own American Revolution. We did not fight the Revolution because we hated Englishmen and wanted to kill them, but because we loved freedom and wanted to establish it. I think it is fair to say, in the light of what that freedom has meant to the world, that the victory won at Yorktown was the greatest victory ever won by force of arms. But this was not because our army was large and formidable. It was because our purpose was so clear, so lofty, and so well defined.

Unhappily this cannot be said of the war of 1914-18. It has become almost a historical truism that that was a war without victory. Of course, it is true that, while we were engaged in it, we thought, or said, that we were fighting for a high purpose. Woodrow Wilson, our Commander in Chief, stated our purpose in eloquent terms. We were fighting to make the world safe for democracy—to make it safe, not just with a slogan, but by accepting a set of principles known as the Fourteen Points, and by setting up a full-fledged international structure to be known as the League of Nations. That was a high purpose, surely. But when the time came to execute it in a peace treaty, a fatal flaw was discovered. We found that we and our allies were not really agreed upon that purpose. On the one hand, some of our allies had entangled themselves in secret treaties; and they were more intent upon carrying out those treaties, and upon pursuing traditional power diplomacy, than upon opening up the new vista that Mr. Wilson had sought to define. And, on the other hand, we ourselves were not so deeply dedicated to our declared purposes as we had led the world to believe. The net result was the abandonment of most of the purposes for which the war had supposedly been fought. Because those purposes were abandoned, that war was denounced by our generation as an enormous and futile slaughter. Millions had lost their lives. But no new idea, no new goal, rose from the ashes of their sacrifice.

Now I think that these considerations lead us inescapably to one conclusion. I think we must conclude that, generally speaking, nothing of importance can be won in peace which has not already been won in the war itself. I say nothing of importance. It is quite true, of course, that many details must be worked out at the peace table and at conferences succeeding the peace table—details which cannot be judiciously worked out under the pressure of war. We—we and our allies, of course —cannot, for instance, stop fighting the Japanese to make a detailed plan of what we intend to do about Burma when victory is won. Nor can we relent in our pressure against Hitler to decide the detailed future of Poland now.

What we must win now, during the war, are the principles. We must know what our line of solution will be. . . .

The people must define their purposes during the war. I have quite deliberately tried to provoke discussion of those purposes among the peoples of the various countries of the world. For I live in a constant dread that this war may end before the people of the world have come to a common understanding of what they fight for and what they hope for after the war is over. I was a soldier in the last war and after that war was over, I saw our bright dreams disappear, our stirring slogans become the jests of the cynical, and all because the fighting peoples did not arrive at any common postwar purposes while they fought. It must be our resolve to see that that does not happen again. . . .

Our leaders, jointly and singly, have expressed some of our common aspirations. One of the finest expressions came from Chiang Kai-shek in a message to the Western world, delivered through the *New York Herald Tribune* Forum on Current Events in New York City last November. He concluded:

China has no desire to replace Western imperialism in Asia with an Oriental imperialism or isolationism of its own or of anyone else. We hold that we must advance from the narrow idea of exclusive alliances and regional blocs, which in the end make for bigger and better wars, to effective organization of world unity. Unless real world co-operation replaces both isolationism and imperialism of whatever form in the new interdependent world of free nations, there will be no lasting security for you or for us.

Add to this Stalin's statement of purpose, which I quoted earlier, a statement on November 6, 1942, on the occasion of the twenty-fifth anniversary of the October Revolution. It is a singularly explicit and exact statement:

Abolition of racial exclusiveness, equality of nations and integrity of their territories, liberation of enslaved nations and restoration of their sovereign rights, the right of every nation to arrange its affairs as it wishes, economic aid to nations that have suffered and assistance to them in attaining their material welfare, restoration of democratic liberties, the destruction of the Hitlerite regime.

Franklin Roosevelt has proclaimed the Four Freedoms and Winston Churchill, with Franklin Roosevelt, has announced to the world the pact of the Atlantic Charter.

The statement of Mr. Stalin and the Atlantic Charter seem to me to have a common fallacy. They forecast the re-creation of western Europe in its old divisions of small nations, each with its own individual political, economic, and military sovereignty. It was this outmoded system that caused millions in Europe to be captivated by Hitler's proposed new order. For even with Hitler tyranny they at least saw the hope of the creation of an area large enough so that the economics of the modern world could successfully function. They had come to realize through bitter experience that the restricted areas of trade imposed by the high walls of a multitude of individual nationalisms, with the consequent manipulations of power politics, made impoverishment and war inevitable.

The re-creation of the small countries of Europe as political units, *yes;* their re-creation as economic and military units, *no*, if we really hope to bring stabilization to western Europe both for its own benefit and for the peace and economic security of the world.

The statement of the Generalissimo, the declaration of Mr. Stalin, the provisions of the Atlantic Charter, and the enunciation of the Four Freedoms are nevertheless each and all signs of great progress and have aroused high hopes around the world.

If the performance, however, does not measure up to the professions or if individual aspirations of nations that make the performance impossible are interposed, the peoples of the world will turn to a corrosive cynicism that will destroy every chance of world order.

People everywhere, articulate and inarticulate people, are watching to see whether the leaders who proclaimed the principles of these documents really meant what they said. . . .

This war that I saw going on all around the world is, in Mr. Stalin's phrase, a war of liberation. It is to liberate some nations from the Nazi or the Japanese Army, and to liberate others from the threat of those armies. On this much we are all agreed. Are we yet agreed that liberation means more than this? Specifically, are the thirty-one United Nations now fighting together agreed that our common job of liberation includes giving to *all* peoples freedom to govern themselves as soon as they are able, and the economic freedom on which all lasting self-government inevitably rests?

It is these two aspects of freedom, I believe, which form the touchstone of our good faith in this war. I believe we must include them both in our idea of the freedom we are fighting for. Otherwise, I am certain we shall not win the peace, and I am not sure we can win the war. . . .

There will be lots of tough problems ahead. And they will differ in different mandates and different colonies. Not all the peoples of the world are ready for freedom, or can defend it, the day after tomorrow. But today they all want some date to work toward, some assurance that the date will be kept. For the future, they do not ask that we solve their problems for them. They are neither so foolish nor so fainthearted. They ask only for the chance to solve their own problems with economic as well as political co-operation. For the peoples of the world intend to be free not only for their political satisfaction, but also for their economic advancement. . . .

America must choose one of three courses after this war: narrow nationalism, which inevitably means the ultimate loss of our own liberty; international imperialism, which means the sacrifice of some other nation's liberty; or the creation of a world in which there shall be an equality of opportunity for every race and every nation. I am convinced the American people will choose, by overwhelming majority, the last of these courses. To make this choice effective, we must win not only the war, but also the peace, and we must start winning it now.

To win this peace three things seem to me necessary—first, we must plan now for peace on a world basis; second, the world must be free, politically and economically, for nations and for men, that peace may exist in it; third, America must play an active, constructive part in freeing it and keeping its peace.

47 ★ *Walter Lippmann, "U.S. War Aims"*

In 1943, Walter Lippmann argued in U.S. Foreign Policy: Shield of the Republic *that no nation should make commitments that its resources would not allow it to fulfill. The United States, he said, could not police the world; but an agreement between the United States,*

England, and Russia could provide the basis for security after the war. In the summer of 1944, Lippmann published U.S. War Aims, in which he criticized those who accepted Wilsonian assumptions. The book, Lippmann later said, was "an open attempt to get away from the One World doctrine." [U.S. War Aims (Boston: Little, Brown and Co., 1944), pp. 158-82. Footnotes omitted. Reprinted by permission of Walter Lippmann.]

War Aims: Then and Now

I would contend that the war aims which I am about to sum up are definite. They say what should be the relations of the United States with its allies and its present enemies.

This is the definite question that the makers of policy have to decide. This is what the people have to make up their minds about. The rest is negotiation, legislation, and administration. Only if the fundamental relationships are determined correctly can the Administration and the Congress have clear objectives for drafting, negotiating, and legislating the agreements and treaties, terms of armistice and of settlement, laws and appropriations covering our military policy and our international relations in the post-war era.

In summary form our war aims are that the United States:—

1. Should consolidate the strategic and diplomatic connections, already existing, of the Atlantic Community: that is to say with the British Commonwealth and Empire, with Pan-America, with France and her empire, with Belgium, the Netherlands, and their colonies, with Luxembourg, Norway, Denmark, Iceland; and should strive to extend them to Portugal, Spain, Italy, Greece, Eire, and Sweden.

2. Should recognize as valid and proper the strategic system of the Russian Orbit, as including within it the states east of Germany and west of the Soviet Union. It should then . . . make known to the Soviet government its view that collaboration in a general world organization will be true and free, or restricted and dubious, depending upon how far the member states—particularly the most powerful ones—maintain at home the democratic liberties which they wish to see advanced abroad.

3. Should recognize that China will be the center of a third strategic system destined to include the whole mainland of Eastern Asia bounded by the frontiers of the Soviet Union and of India, and that the end of the war with Japan will inaugurate a new epoch in Chinese-American relations. Though we must be deeply concerned with the maintenance

of peace in Asia, we can no longer be, as we have been from the time of John Hay, specially committed to China. For while we could be the special champions of China when the center of China's activity was still along her coasts, in the interior of Asia we can have no such commitment. For it is beyond our reach.

4. Should recognize that in time the Moslem and the Hindu nations of North Africa, the Middle East, and Southern Asia will form regional systems of their own.

5. Should make it the primary aim of the Far East settlement that Japan shall not hold the balance of power in the Far East among China, the Soviet Union, and the United States; should make it the primary aim of the German settlement that Germany shall not hold the balance of power between the Atlantic Community and the Russian Orbit.

6. Should recognize that the general aim of any lasting settlement of a war of aggression is to extinguish the war party and to protect the peace party, by making the defeat irrevocable and the peace acceptable.

It is my conviction that by following these lines of policy, the nations can come to rest in a long peace. Here is an order of power in which the vital interests of all the states capable of waging a great war are secured and are in equilibrium. It is not a mere diplomatic mechanism based on legal fictions, and then superimposed upon the real action of national states. It is a definite order of power among the national states of the world today: it is definite because it requires them to fix and stabilize their foreign policy with their neighbors. They do not surrender their sovereignty; they do reform their unpredictability and their vacillation, and they do forgo their right of arbitrary diplomatic maneuver in international relations. And I hold that only upon the stable foundations of such an ordered peace can a successful universal society be established.

The Error of 1919

This has not been, I realize, the prevailing American view since the days of President Wilson. He believed that a universal society like the League of Nations could be charged with the making and the keeping of peace. In this inquiry I take the radically different view, that held at the close, though not at the beginning, of the First World War by Theodore Roosevelt in this country, and by Georges Clemenceau abroad. It is that the deeper issues which are likely to disturb the peace must be settled not by the universal society, but in order that the universal society may have a chance to live and prosper. I do not believe that the security of the vital interests of the United States can be, should be, or will be entrusted to the collective security which a new and tentative international institution can be counted on to provide.

For ourselves, in the world as it is, we are certain to rely first upon our own armed power and national strength, then upon our natural allies, and then upon a general world organization. We shall not look upon the general organization as a substitute for our own measures of security but as a means of reinforcing them. If that is so, we must not expect Great Britain, the Soviet Union, China, France, or any other country to place a greater reliance upon collective security than we ourselves do. We shall wish to enter the universal society, having first made ourselves as secure as we can. They will do likewise.

It is now agreed among the governments that the general world organization, which the four great powers have promised to establish, is not to be charged with settling this war. That, as the Moscow Agreement states, is the task of the four principal Allies consulting with members of the United Nations. But it is widely supposed, and perhaps even implied in the Agreement, that the general organization will in the near future become the guardian of the peace of the world. I am contending that we cannot rely upon it to do that. To prevent another war of aggression by our present enemies, we must rely upon the terms of peace—and upon pacts which bind together the Allies to enforce the terms of peace. Even less should we conceive the general world organization as being charged with preventing some other great theoretical war in which, let us say, the Soviet Union, China, Britain, and America are enemies. Quite the contrary, I think: a war among the founders of the universal society must be prevented in order that the society may survive. It cannot be prevented by the rules and procedures of the universal society but only by the direct recognition of national interests and their mutual accommodation. The world organization cannot police the policemen. If that is what it is supposed to do, it will not only fail, as did the League, but it will almost certainly excite tensions and alignments which will hasten its failure.

This was, in essence, the French view in 1919, and we must now admit, I believe, that Clemenceau was right and that Wilson was wrong. . . .

The organized power which wins the war must be used to win the peace. It can bring to an end the frightful wars of our age. If it cannot, then nothing can, certainly not some pale, thin, abstract, generalized blueprint of a mechanism.

The Work of a Universal Society

The true function of the universal society is to facilitate intercourse among nations already at peace. This task—of maintaining standards and instituting reforms, which were nonpolitical and more concerned with individual than with national security—the League of Nations performed exceedingly well. It would have done it better and better if only the world had remained at peace, and when peace comes again, the work will be resumed and expanded.

If the new world society is not burdened with the task of preventing great wars among the great powers, it can do much to prevent, regulate, and compose the disputes that are not directly and closely related to the greatest issues of war and peace. We know that hard cases do not make good law; it is in the treatment of the easier cases that principles of international comity will develop, and decisions will be rendered that become precedents, expanding the common law of the nations. . . .

Let us not be so naïve as to think that the great issues of war and peace, upon which hangs the life of nations, will or can be settled by public debates and public voting in an international assembly. Matters of life and death cannot be submitted to a conglomerate parliament of mankind. The critical decisions must in any event be threshed out first in quiet and in confidence by those who have the responsibility because they have the power. . . .

The decision not to charge the world society with the task of preventing war by policing the world will, I believe, make it more likely that war will be prevented. For it will fix the responsibility where alone it can be discharged—upon the governments of the great powers and their neighbors with whom they are allied. There will be no pretense, and no escape by means of the pretense, that the responsibility for preventing war is anywhere else than where it really is: in the great military states themselves. . . .

The Wilsonian Principles: The Moral Order

It is indubitably true, as Wilson had the vision to see, that the international society must rest at last upon the acceptance of common principles of conduct. But they must be principles which men can believe in and can live by. The Wilsonian principles did not and cannot meet this test. They are negative rules which, though meant to prohibit aggression and tyranny, in fact prohibit national states from making the provisions which will insure their own survival against aggression and tyranny. To end the struggle for power Wilson sought to make the nations powerless. The Wilsonian principles stipulate that the nations should disarm themselves physically and politically and then entrust their independence and their vital interests to an assembly of debating diplomats. This is like arguing that because the Bible says the love of money is the root of all evil, none should work for money and all should depend on the charity of their neighbors.

The cynicism which corroded the democracies in the interval between the two German wars was engendered by a moral order which was in fact a moral frustration. Field Marshal Smuts overlooked this when he pronounced the judgment that not Wilson but humanity failed at Paris. The moralists at Paris gave humanity a code of morality which no one could observe, which, in so far as its prohibitions had influence in disarming the nations, disaggregating alliances, and disrupting great states, was a preparation not for peace under the law but for aggression in the midst of anarchy. The moral code failed because it was not a good moral code.

We too shall fail to find a moral basis for the international order if we do not discern and then correct the spiritual error which underlies the Wilsonian misconception. It is the error of forgetting that we are men and of thinking that we are gods. We are not gods. We do not have the omniscience to discover a new moral law and the omnipotence to impose it upon mankind. When we draw up lists of general principles which we say are universal, to which we mean to hold everyone, we are indulging in a fantasy. We are imagining ourselves as beings who are above and outside mankind, detached from the concrete realities of life itself, and able to govern the world by fiat. But in fact we are inside the human world. We are mere mortals with limited power and little universal wisdom.

We shall collaborate best with other nations if we start with the homely fact that their families and their homes, their villages and lands, their countries and their own ways, their altars, their flags, and their hearths—not charters, covenants, blueprints, and generalities—are what men live for and will, if it is necessary, die for.

A sound moral code of international life will not prohibit men from relying at last upon their own virtue in defending and preserving the things they cherish more than life itself. It must not ask them to hazard their vital interests on schemes which, if they failed, would ruin them. A sound moral code must be rooted deeply in the things men live and die for. It must be the means of conserving these real things, and it must be so cogently, so candidly, so sincerely devoted to these deeply human and substantial ends that the code itself evokes their instinctive assent and their natural loyalty.

No code of international conduct can do this, I believe, which does not derive from the view that the world order can eventually be formed only by organizing from the national state, ascending through the regional neighborhood, and then to the larger communities and to a concert of great communities.

48 ★ *Franklin D. Roosevelt,* The Postwar World

The memory of Woodrow Wilson's defeat over the League of Nations haunted Franklin Roosevelt and other advocates of world organization. Accordingly, the President tried to avoid a postwar slump in idealism by stressing the difficulties inherent in peace-making, and he sought to forestall Republican opposition by removing the United Nations from the realm of partisan controversy. In a press conference on May 30, 1944, the President revealed some of the changes in perspective that had occurred since 1919. [Samuel I. Rosenman, ed., The Public Papers and Addresses of Franklin D. Roosevelt (New York: Harper and Bros., 1950), Vol. XIII, 140-42. Reprinted by permission.]

QUESTION: Mr. President, when you were in the Navy Department as Assistant Secretary, I was not a newspaperman, but if my mind serves me right, at that time you supported President Wilson on the League of Nations. I wonder if you could say anything as to what you think about that now?

THE PRESIDENT: Well, I think I was quite right in supporting it at the time.

QUESTION: How do you feel about it now?

THE PRESIDENT: About a new League of Nations?

QUESTION: Yes, sir.

THE PRESIDENT: Well, you know that we are working toward a unity of the United Nations toward the prevention, if we can humanly help it, of another World War. Of course, it was a new experience for us in those days—brand new. It was going to be a war to end wars, and it was to be done through this altruistic unity of all the Nations, of which we were going to be part. We hoped that there would never be any more wars.

Well, you are older than you were then. Probably, in those days, you would have been in favor of the theory of ending all wars. Today, we are a little older; we have gone through some pretty rough times together. And perhaps we are not saying that we can devise a method of ending all wars for all time. Some of us—I don't think I include myself in this—are a little more cynical than we were then. Some of us—and I don't think I include myself—are a little more foolish-minded domestically than we were when we were twenty-five years younger.

And so we have an objective today, and that is to join with the other Nations of the world not in such a way that some other Nation would decide whether we were to build a new dam on the Conestoga Creek, but for general world peace in setting up some machinery of talking things over with other Nations, without taking away the independence of the United States in any shape, manner, or form, or destroying—what's the other word?—the *integrity* of the United States in any shape, manner, or form; with the objective of working so closely that if some Nation in the world started to run amuck, or some combination of Nations started to run amuck, and seeks to grab territory or invade its neighbors, that there would be a unanimity of opinion that the time to stop them was before they got started; that is, all the other Nations who weren't in with them.

And, in a sense, the League of Nations had that very, very great purpose. It got dreadfully involved in American politics, instead of being regarded as a nonpartisan subject.

And that is why, in this particular year, the Secretary of State and I have been working very closely together, and we have been working in conferences with the duly constituted Constitutional machinery of Government, which in this case happens to be the Senators on the Foreign Relations Committee—four from each party. And, so far, the conversations with them have been conducted on the very high level of nonpartisanship. So far, they have worked very well. . . .

But let me emphasize that both the Secretary of State and I—and, I think, the Senators—have been trying to look at this thing in a spirit of nonpartisanship, thinking about a hundred and thirty-five million Americans, and thinking about a great many small Nations, as well as the bigger Nations, who at this stage are directly involved.

After we get through talking—what I call the first draft—we will talk, of course, with all the other Nations of the world. . . .

QUESTION: What you mean then, if I interpret what you said correctly, is that you are not following the pattern of the former League of Nations, but you are seeking for a new pattern as applied to latter-day questions?

THE PRESIDENT: Well, you can't follow the old pattern, because obviously conditions are entirely different from those days in 1919—entirely different. We are proceeding with a good deal more experience than we had then on a 1944 pattern—at least what we think is a 1944 pattern—rather than a 1919 pattern. . . .